TRASHING THE PLANET

EXAMINING OUR GLOBAL GARBAGE GLUT

STUART A. KALLEN

TWENTY-FIRST CENTURY BOOKS / MINNEAPOLIS

To all the students throughout the world working to stop mountains of junk from burying Planet Earth and searching for creative solutions to the garbage crisis. And let's not forget the dedicated scientists, biologists, environmentalists, garbologists, and just plain folks working every day to solve the trash problem.

Twenty-First Century Books
A division of Lerner Publishing Group, Inc.
241 First Avenue North
Minneapolis, MN 55401 USA

For reading levels and more information, look up this title at www.lernerbooks.com.

Main body text set in Adobe Garamond Pro 11/15.
Typeface provided by Adobe Systems.

Library of Congress Cataloging-in-Publication Data

Names: Kallen, Stuart A., 1955– author.
Title: Trashing the planet : examining our global garbage glut / Stuart A. Kallen.
Description: Minneapolis : Twenty-First Century Books, [2017] | Includes bibliographical references and index.
Identifiers: LCCN 2016033032 (print) | LCCN 2016033466 (ebook) | ISBN 9781512413144 (lb : alk. paper) | ISBN 9781512448665 (eb pdf)
Subjects: LCSH: Refuse and refuse disposal—Juvenile literature.
Classification: LCC TD792 .K346 2017 (print) | LCC TD792 (ebook) | DDC 363.72/85—dc23

LC record available at https://lccn.loc.gov/2016033032

Manufactured in the United States of America
1-39767-21311-12/13/2016

CONTENTS

CHAPTER 1

FROM RAGS AND BONES TO PLASTIC DISASTER

On September 15, 2015, a mega-storm dumped a record-breaking 2.4 inches (6 centimeters) of rain on drought-stricken Los Angeles in just one day. In Southern California, the first big storm of the fall usually comes after a summer of little rainfall and brings what locals call the "first flush." Like the flushing of a giant toilet, the rainwater courses through LA's urban storm sewers and flood control channels, picking up tons of garbage along the way. The rainwater carries the trash into rivers, which flow into the Pacific Ocean. Most of the trash is plastic: single-use water bottles, shopping bags, toys, athletic shoes, car parts,

Heavy rains each fall carry trash from the streets and sewers of Los Angeles into rivers and then into the Pacific Ocean. Discarded plastic, Styrofoam, and other debris end up on beaches and bob in waters offshore.

electronic devices, beer and soda coolers, and countless other plastic-based consumer goods.

The first flush of 2015 attracted a handful of trash pickers to Seal Beach, south of Los Angeles, where the San Gabriel River flows into the Pacific Ocean. The pickers searched for items they could sell at swap meets or garage sales. Katie Allen is the director of Algalita Marine Research and Education, which studies the impact of plastic pollution on beaches and oceans. She visited Seal Beach after the 2015 first flush and talked to the trash pickers. Allen remarked, "Although their relationship with the first flush is purely business, every single picker I interviewed . . . was profoundly disheartened by the mess." She continued, "Much of the debris was completely worthless, and [most of it] remained on the beach."

The City of Los Angeles works to prevent garbage from washing into the ocean during the first flush. City workers clean storm drains before seasonal rains begin in the fall. Consumers recycle plastic on trash pickup days. Yet garbage still piles up. After the 2015 first flush, many sandy California beaches—glorified in rock songs, books, and movies—turned into trash dumps. And the garbage is more than an eyesore. Over time, ocean waves will carry the trash into the Pacific Ocean. There, sunlight, rain, and waves will break it up into small pieces. As the plastic and other synthetic (human-made) materials decompose, some of them will release poisonous chemicals into the air and water.

The scene at Seal Beach after the first flush is a microcosm of the worldwide garbage crisis. Cities across the United States and nearly every other country on Earth have similar garbage problems. Every day, manufacturers create countless products to sell to millions of consumers. And just about everything comes packaged inside and secured with instant trash: cardboard boxes, plastic boxes, plastic and Styrofoam wrappers, plastic bottles, plastic sheeting, rubber bands, twist ties, and more. Consumers toss most containers and wrappers into the trash. Even the products themselves often end up in the trash. When toys and electric appliances break, many people simply toss them and buy new ones. It's easy and cheap to do so. On a global scale, humans create around 2.6 trillion pounds (1.2 trillion kilograms) of garbage a year.

In the face of the garbage crisis, the United States, other wealthy nations, and local governments around the world are trying to contain the accumulation of trash. Many cities run recycling programs, collecting plastic, glass, and metal containers; old newspapers, magazines, and scrap paper; and cardboard. The cities sell recycled materials to businesses that turn them into new containers, fresh sheets of paper, and even products such as park benches. Even so, Americans recycle only about 30 percent of their trash every year.

In the United States, trash put out for curbside pickup rather than recycling usually goes to landfills or incinerators, where the trash is either buried under layers of soil or burned. However, the rotting garbage in landfills frequently leaks toxic liquids that can seep into and poison groundwater. Garbage-burning incinerators release toxic gases through their smokestacks, polluting the air we breathe. In many poor nations, cities have no curbside trash or recycling programs at all. There, people simply pile garbage onto gigantic heaps outside, burn it, or dump it into local rivers.

ANCIENT TRASH HEAPS

The global garbage glut is a relatively new problem. For thousands of years, everything humans produced came from the natural world around them.

Many US cities dispose of garbage by burning it in big incinerators. At this incinerator in Harrisburg, Pennsylvania, a mechanical claw grabs garbage and moves it to a furnace.

Ancient humans made knives, axes, and other tools out of shells, animal bones, wood, and stones. Potters shaped clay into containers to hold food and water. Other ancient craftspeople wove reeds, leaves, and twigs into baskets. They used plant fibers and the skins and wool of animals to make clothing. All these materials are biodegradable—when they decompose, they break down into tiny, harmless particles. In fact, the particles actually benefit the environment. They contain minerals and other substances that enrich the soil and provide nutrition for plants.

Early peoples used their tools, containers, and fabrics until they broke or tore. They tossed items that couldn't be mended or reused onto trash heaps on the outskirts of their settlements. Some of the trash, such as baskets and clothing, decomposed quickly. Other trash, such as bones, shells, stone tools, and pieces of glazed pottery, decomposed very slowly, over thousands of years. Yet none of these items polluted the air, land, or water. Modern archaeologists study middens, or ancient trash heaps. The shells, pottery, and other long-lasting items found there help archaeologists determine how people prepared food, what types of tools and weapons they used, and much more about daily life in ancient times.

CITY LIFE

The world's first cities emerged in the ancient Middle East in about 3500 BCE. Historians think that ancient city dwellers simply tossed their garbage—including human waste, animal waste, and animal carcasses— into streets or rivers. Over the centuries, as cities grew larger, garbage became an increasingly worrisome problem. Piles of waste attracted flies, rats, and other pests that spread diseases to humans.

During the Industrial Revolution—which began in the late eighteenth century in Great Britain—companies started to use power-driven machinery to produce goods. Although craftspeople still made many items by hand, more and more products came from large urban factories. With industrialization, which eventually spread to other parts of Europe and to North America, cities got bigger and dirtier.

But even in industrialized cities, most individuals did not produce much garbage. Goods were expensive, and citizens were thrifty. They made much of their own food, clothing, tools, and cleaning supplies at home. Nothing was wasted. Housewives used food scraps to make soup or fed them to domestic animals such as pigs and chickens. Families handed down tools, housewares, furniture, and clothing from one generation to the next. When clothing items ripped or wore out, women mended them by hand or used the scraps of cloth as diapers or rags.

If an item couldn't be repaired or reused, it could be sold for a few pennies. In cities, towns, and rural areas, peddlers called ragmen or rag-and-bone men went door-to-door in horse-drawn carts, buying old clothes, scrap metal, scrap paper, cooking grease, and animal bones. They sold the materials to businesses that recycled them into new products. For instance, papermakers shredded old cloth, mixed it with water, and

mashed it into a pulp, which they then formed into sheets of paper. Some craftspeople turned old cooking grease into candles and soap. Other workers ground up animal bones and sold them to farmers as fertilizer.

Eventually, industrialization changed the way consumers obtained household items, especially in the United States. In the mid-nineteenth century, US manufacturers began to produce more and more goods for the consumer market. Instead of making everything at home, Americans could visit corner stores and department stores to buy clothing, foods, soaps, and housewares. Most products had very little packaging then. Consumers usually bought food and cleaning products in bulk and carried their goods home in cloth bags.

This engraving from 1868 shows New York City rag pickers selling salvaged materials to a scrap merchant. Sometimes called ragmen or rag-and-bone men, recyclers made money by collecting unwanted materials from households and reselling them. This was long before the era of city-run recycling programs.

However, the businesses that produced the new consumer goods contributed to the dirt and grime of cities. Factories powered their machinery by burning coal and petroleum. Smoke and soot belched from factory smokestacks, polluting the air and water. Human sewage added to the filth. While some nineteenth-century cities built sewer systems and some wealthy people installed flush toilets and indoor plumbing in their homes, many city dwellers relieved themselves in outhouses and chamber pots. Waste often seeped from outhouses into the surrounding soil and waterways, and citizens often emptied chamber pots by simply dumping the contents outside.

As cities grew bigger, dirtier, and more crowded, trash began to pile up. Some city officials realized that garbage was a threat to public health. They hired workers to pick up residents' trash and haul it to dumps on the edge of town. Usually just open pits, these places reeked, and they attracted rats and other pests.

Meanwhile, US companies picked up the pace of manufacturing. In the early twentieth century, using assembly-line production, factories churned out mass-produced clothing, housewares, cosmetics, canned foods, and electric appliances. In magazines such as *Ladies' Home Journal* and the *Saturday Evening Post*, advertisers promised Americans that they would find health and happiness with new hair-care products, instant baking mixes, presliced bread, vacuum cleaners, toasters, radios, toothpaste, deodorants, and nail polish. To attract shoppers' attention, manufacturers placed the new products inside colorful and decorative packaging. The containers and wrappers included cans, cardboard boxes, aluminum foil, paper, and cellophane (an early form of plastic).

With mass production and more stores, the new goods were affordable and easy to purchase. US families no longer reused household materials the way earlier generations had. They began to toss empty containers, food scraps, and other garbage into the waste bin rather than upcycling them. More big cities began to provide curbside garbage pickup. But instead of just taking trash to open dumps, haulers took it to

By the early decades of the twentieth century, access to mass-produced goods had become a reality for most American consumers. They bought manufactured food products, cleaning supplies, toiletry items, and other items from stores rather than making them at home. The shift led to a significant increase in the amount of trash Americans produced every year. This 1936 picture by acclaimed US photographer Berenice Abbott shows the display window of an A&P grocery store in New York City.

large incinerators or to facilities called sanitary landfills. There, operators covered layers of trash with alternating layers of soil. Burying the garbage helped cut down on rats and odors. More and more cities built sewage systems to carry off and treat human waste. Indoor toilets became commonplace in big cities.

But trash removal and sanitation was not uniform across the United States. In many places, citizens still carted their trash to open dumps on the outskirts of town. In other areas, residents burned their own garbage in backyard or basement incinerators, releasing toxic smoke into the air. Many Americans still used outhouses well into the twentieth century.

THE PLASTIC AGE

Besides selling new consumer products, manufacturers took advantage of new materials. These included celluloid, a plastic made from plant fiber, nitric acid, and camphor (a substance found in the wood and bark of camphor trees). Businesses used celluloid to make items such as combs and hairbrushes, dolls, and photographic film. Invented by US chemist Leo Baekeland in 1909, Bakelite was a kind of plastic made from the chemicals carbolic acid and formaldehyde. Manufacturers turned to Bakelite to produce telephones, radio casings, buttons, and costume jewelry. Starting in the late 1920s, chemists began to develop stronger and more flexible plastics, including polystyrene, polyester, polyvinyl chloride, and polyethylene terephthalate. Many of the new plastics were made from petrochemicals, or chemicals derived from petroleum or natural gas.

Manufacturers launched advertising campaigns to sell the wonders of plastic to the public, and the advertising worked. Consumers came to believe that plastic was a miracle substance, and in some ways, it is. Plastic is lightweight and inexpensive. It can be molded into just about any shape. It can be rigid and strong or soft and flexible. Plastic wrapping keeps food fresh by blocking out harmful bacteria. Plastic beverage bottles are much lighter and cheaper than glass bottles and do not shatter like glass. Some plastic fibers are even strong enough to stop bullets.

In the 1950s, companies used plastic to make plates and cups, toys, clothing, office supplies, household appliances, and thousands of other products. Americans filled their homes with materials bearing names such as Tupperware, Formica, and Naugahyde. Manufacturers also used petrochemicals to make synthetic paints, adhesives, insulation, cleaning supplies, cosmetics, fertilizers, and pesticides.

The new products were popular with both consumers and businesses. But they came with a downside. Because plastic and other synthetics were inexpensive and abundant, consumers didn't hesitate to throw them away when they were no longer needed. The materials quickly ended up in landfills and incinerators.

BLACK MONDAY

On July 26, 1943, a black haze of noxious pollution enveloped downtown Los Angeles, California. The thick smoke blotted out sunlight. It left thousands of city residents coughing and choking as tears flowed from their stinging eyes. Pedestrians clutched handkerchiefs to their faces, hoping in vain to filter out the airborne toxins. The day became known as Black Monday.

Los Angelenos called the pollution smog, a combination of fog and smoke that often settles over Southern California. A ring of high mountains surrounds the Los Angeles Basin, trapping smog within the city. In the 1940s and 1950s, this toxic pollution choked Los Angeles residents on at least two hundred days a year.

Most residents blamed cars and factories for creating the Black Monday smog, but the problem was actually caused by household trash. At the time, many of LA residents burned garbage in backyard incinerators nicknamed Smokey Joes. This method of garbage disposal added 500 tons (454 metric tons) of sooty, toxic pollution to the air every day. The smog was so bad that Los Angeles residents could not dry their clothes outdoors because black soot often rained down from the skies.

When scientists pointed out the problems caused by Smokey Joes, many city residents refused to give up garbage burning. They could pay a fee to have the city haul their trash to a landfill, but many did not want to pay. In 1957 Los Angeles finally passed a law that banned backyard trash burning. A $500 fine awaited anyone who fired up a Smokey Joe.

Smog hangs over downtown Los Angeles in the 1940s. The bulk of the city's air pollution in this era stemmed from burning home garbage. Millions of city residents burned their trash in backyard incinerators called Smokey Joes.

Unlike natural materials such as wood, animal fibers, and plant resins, the plastics and other synthetics pouring into US landfills and incinerators in the mid-twentieth century didn't break down into harmless substances. Modern scientists tell us that petroleum-based plastic never really goes away. It simply breaks apart into tiny pieces too small to be seen with the naked eye. Scientists note that many kinds of plastic release toxic chemicals as they decay. If burned in an incinerator, plastic and other synthetics produce different kinds of dioxin. These toxic chemicals can cause cancer and other serious health problems—although that was unknown when plastics first became popular in the mid-twentieth century.

CLEAN AND GREEN

In the 1960s, people around the globe became alarmed about growing levels of environmental contamination. Pollution from cars and industry was fouling the air in many cities. Many large industries were dumping

RECYCLING THEN AND NOW

Recycling is creating new items from used materials. Humans have been recycling and reusing goods for centuries. Archaeologists say that as long ago as the fourth century BCE, the Romans and other ancient groups melted metal jewelry and coins to make weapons of war.

In more recent times, the US government instituted a recycling program during World War II (1939–1945). US manufacturers needed materials such as steel, aluminum, and rubber to produce tanks, airplanes, guns, and bombs for the fighting forces. The US government launched a massive advertising campaign, encouraging Americans to donate old household goods to be recycled into weapons. In nearly every neighborhood, schoolchildren collected old pots and pans, car parts, tin cans, scrap paper, garden hoses, and tires from their neighbors. Kids even collected used cooking grease for making ammunition.

In the twenty-first century, the benefits of recycling are well known. Recycling reduces the need to build more landfills and incinerators while conserving natural resources like timber (used to make paper) and metals. Despite the benefits of recycling, the EPA estimates that Americans recycle only about 30 percent of the garbage that can be recycled. Europeans recycle about 36 percent of their trash. Most poor nations have no formal recycling programs.

hazardous waste, such as industrial chemicals and radioactive materials (waste from nuclear weapons and nuclear power production that emits deadly radiation), into lakes and rivers or onto vacant lands. US biologist Rachel Carson's groundbreaking book *Silent Spring* (1962) explained how pesticides—chemicals used to kill insects that harm crops—were fouling the air and water and also killing birds and fish. In the United States, the pressure for reform was so great that the US government passed a series of laws designed to reduce pollution and protect the environment.

The push to clean up the environment extended to waste management. By the mid-1960s, more and more US cities were disposing of trash in incinerators or sanitary landfills. Yet some towns still maintained dangerous open dumps. In 1965 the US Congress passed the Solid Waste Disposal Act. This law established guidelines for the safe collection and disposal of trash from households and businesses. The act was designed to help state and local governments switch from dumps to sanitary landfills or incinerators.

In 1970 US president Richard Nixon directed Congress to create the Environmental Protection Agency (EPA), a federal organization tasked with protecting the nation's environment. The EPA's work included ensuring that landfills, incinerators, and other garbage facilities did not contaminate air, land, or water. In 1976 Congress passed the Resource Conservation and Recovery Act (RCRA). Implemented by the EPA, the RCRA set guidelines for the safe transportation, treatment, and storage of toxic (or hazardous) waste. This material includes medical waste, heavy metals such as lead and mercury, and poisonous chemicals from farms, homes, and automobiles. The waste takes the form of sludge, solids, and liquids.

Also in the 1970s, many cities set up curbside recycling programs to reduce the amount of newspapers, glass jars and bottles, and aluminum cans heading to landfills and incinerators. By the 1980s, most US recycling programs were collecting plastic as well. During the 1990s, many European nations created recycling programs.

In the 1970s, cities in the United States launched programs to recycle used glass, paper, and metal. In the following decades, recycling programs began to collect plastic containers as well. European cities also started recycling in the late twentieth century. In this photo, bales of crushed plastic travel along a conveyor belt at a recycling facility in Switzerland.

The new laws and programs helped ensure that trash would be handled safely in the future, but many sites in the United States and around the world were already contaminated by toxic waste. In 1980 Congress passed the Comprehensive Environmental Response, Compensation, and Liability Act (CERCLA), commonly called the Superfund. Overseen by the EPA, the Superfund prohibits the discharging of toxic waste into the environment and forces polluters to clean up toxic sites by digging up contaminated soil and removing the hazardous waste.

DROWNING IN GARBAGE

The new laws and regulations helped control the processing of garbage in the United States, but they could do nothing to slow the creation of

SUPERFUND SUPERSLOW

One of every four Americans lives within 4 miles (6.4 km) of a Superfund site, but cleanup is slow. When Congress created the Superfund in 1980, the law stated that the polluter pays for cleanup. This means that the companies, organizations, and individuals that contaminated a site must fund the cleanup efforts. But cleaning up toxic waste is so expensive that many companies go out of business rather than spend millions of dollars to clean up their toxic trash.

In 1995 the provision that allowed the Superfund to collect money from polluters expired, and Congress failed to reauthorize it. This left the Superfund to rely only on money from the federal budget to clean up the hazardous sites. Since 2010 Congress has allocated $1.26 billion a year to the Superfund program, about one-quarter of the money the program had in 1995. This decrease has caused a dramatic reduction in the number of Superfund sites being treated.

According to Kaley Beins and Stephen Lester of the Center for Health, Environment and Justice, "Decreased funding and the slowdown of the cleanup of Superfund sites have resulted in increased toxic exposures and health threats to communities across America. . . . Without industry fees to replenish Superfund, there is simply not enough money to do the critical job of cleaning up hundreds of abandoned toxic waste sites and the American taxpayers are unfairly burdened by paying 100% of the annual costs." As of July 2016, only about one-third of the nation's 1,328 Superfund sites had been completely cleaned.

garbage. Between 1960 and 2015, the US population nearly doubled. Meanwhile, the amount of trash produced in the United States more than quadrupled—from 88 million tons (80 million metric tons) of garbage in 1960 to 390 million tons (354 million metric tons) in 2013.

In 2016 the United States produces more garbage than any other single country. China is the world's second-largest garbage producer, creating 190 million tons (172 million metric tons) of waste per year. Few Chinese cities pick up residential trash. Much of it sits in dumps on the outskirts of towns. Around the world, in most poor nations, citizens burn trash in open pits; leave it in forests, fields, and roadside ditches; toss it into rivers and lakes; or pitch it into the ocean.

Household garbage includes food waste, plastic packaging, electronics, clothing, and yard waste. In addition, US manufacturers produce about

42 billion pounds (19 billion kg) of chemical waste each day. And despite US laws regulating the disposal of toxic chemicals, many of them make their way into soil, lakes, and rivers. From there, they can enter the food humans eat (through food crops that take up the chemicals into their roots or through the meat of beef cattle and other livestock that eat contaminated plants). They also end up in the water we drink. Research shows that at least six million Americans have been exposed to drinking water that contains toxic chemicals. In 2016 at least one-quarter of China's rivers were so contaminated with toxic waste that citizens could not safely use the water for drinking, irrigating crops, or both.

NO IMPACT MAN

While the global garbage crisis can seem overwhelming, individuals are not powerless in the face of mountains of trash. Those who study the

Many poor nations have no curbside garbage or recycling pickup. People simply toss their trash into open dumps or into rivers. The garbage in this photo lines the banks of a waterway in New Delhi, India.

science of garbage, called garbologists, say that solving the trash problem begins at home. Consumers can reduce waste by purchasing less. They can also choose to buy used or refurbished electronics, clothes, and other products instead of brand-new ones. (Thrifting is fun!) They can hold swap meets with friends to trade items and can donate the leftovers to thrift shops. They can bring reusable bags to the grocery store. They can say no to plastic bags at the grocery checkout line and recycle the bags they do use at local supermarkets. Citizens can volunteer to clean up trash along roadsides and beaches. They can bring reusable mugs to coffee shops. They can pack their own lunches in nonplastic containers. They can bike, walk, or take public transportation to school and to their jobs to cut down on car exhaust. Dozens of websites contain other ideas for reducing, reusing, upcycling, and recycling.

Many consumers have chosen to limit their participation in the throwaway economy. They include New Yorker Colin Beavan and his family, who tried to live for a year without generating any garbage. Beavan, known as No Impact Man, stopped buying beverages in cans and plastic bottles, coffee in disposable cups, and foods in plastic packaging. Instead, he drank from city water fountains, grew food at a local community garden, and bought other food in bulk, carrying it home in reusable containers. Beavan's blog, noimpactman.com, read by thousands, gives tips about reducing consumer impact on the environment. Beavan and his family are not the only ones aspiring to a zero-impact lifestyle. He and other zero-waste families hope to inspire millions—or even billions—of consumers and cities to become no-impact global citizens.

CHAPTER 2

THE UNITED STATES OF TRASH

Americans have a love affair with trash. The United States has about 5 percent of the world's population but generates 30 percent of its garbage. According to a 2008 study by Columbia University in New York, the average American throws away about 7.1 pounds (3.2 kg) of waste each day, every day. That adds up to about 102 tons (93 metric tons) of trash over a person's lifetime. Edward Humes, author of the book *Garbology: Our Dirty Love Affair with Trash*, says, "Each of our bodies may occupy only one cemetery plot when we're done with this world, but a single person's 102-ton trash legacy will require the equivalent

A sanitation worker loads trash from a Dumpster into the back of a garbage truck. Every year, Americans generate more than 390 million tons (354 million metric tons) of garbage.

[space] of 1,100 graves. Much of the refuse will outlast any grave marker, pharaoh's pyramid or modern skyscraper."

Once we've put our garbage cans out on the curb, trash collectors load our waste into garbage trucks, compress it, and haul it away. And it takes a lot of trucks to handle US garbage. In fact, each day Americans throw away enough stuff to fill sixty-three thousand garbage trucks. According to Humes, one of every six big trucks in the United States is a garbage truck.

New York City, the largest city in the United States, relies on both trucks and trains to handle its garbage. Every day, such vehicles leave the city loaded with 12,000 tons (10,886 metric tons) of garbage headed for out-of-state landfills. "How much is 12,000 tons a day?" asks Humes. "That's like throwing away sixty-two Boeing 747 jumbo jets daily, or driving 8,730 new Honda Civics into a landfill each morning."

SANITARY LANDFILLS

The end of the line for most US garbage—about 70 percent of it—is the sanitary landfill. The EPA oversees US landfills and enforces numerous regulations governing their design and operations. US landfills vary in size. Some measure hundreds of feet in depth and cover several hundred acres of land

SHRINK-WRAPPING TEXAS

Pulitzer Prize–winning journalist Edward Humes has compiled many statistics about American waste. Humes writes that each year Americans discard the following:

- 5.7 million tons (5.2 million metric tons) of carpet
- 19 billion pounds (8.6 billion kg) of polystyrene peanuts (Styrofoam)
- thirty-five billion plastic bottles
- forty billion plastic knives, forks, and spoons
- 4.5 million tons (4 million metric tons) of office paper
- enough wood to heat fifty million homes for twenty years
- enough plastic film to shrink-wrap Texas

HARMFUL E-WASTE

Electronic waste, or e-waste, includes any discarded device that runs on electric current or batteries. Every day Americans throw out about 130,000 computers, 426,000 cell phones, and countless other electronic gadgets. The devices usually come in plastic cases, which can sit in landfills for hundreds of years before decomposing. In addition, components inside the devices contain some of the most dangerous toxins on Earth. For instance, the circuit boards inside computers and cell phones hold a wide array of dangerous chemicals, including lead, copper, mercury, cadmium, zinc, chromium, and barium. Americans recycle only about 12 percent of their e-waste. Much of the rest ends up in landfills, where the toxic chemicals become part of the leachate.

The batteries that power many electronic devices also add to garbage problems. Every year Americans toss out about three billion batteries. Batteries contain toxins such as nickel, lead, cadmium, and lithium and make up 20 percent of the hazardous waste found in landfills. When the batteries decompose, they emit gases that contribute to air pollution and climate change. The chemicals from batteries also join with leachate in a landfill, and when landfills leak, the toxins from batteries can contaminate air, water, and soil.

Many US communities have established e-waste and battery recycling programs. Investigate the options in your town, and be sure to use them.

Electronic waste (e-waste) contains hazardous heavy metals and other toxins. This photograph shows an e-waste scrapyard in Hamburg, Germany.

Engineers design landfills to hold garbage and to keep it from contaminating groundwater, soil, and air. On the bottom and on all sides, a thick layer of compacted clay lines the typical landfill, with a polyethylene liner inside that. Above the liner, most landfills include several layers of absorbent substances, such as soil, pea gravel, or synthetic fabric. Landfills are open to the air at the top.

Each day a typical big city landfill might receive 20 tons (18 metric tons) of trash. At the end of the day, massive bulldozers called BOMAGs (named for the German maker of the vehicles, Bopparder Maschinenbau-Gesellschaft) cover that day's new garbage with 1 foot (0.3 meters) of soil, chipped wood, or another plant-based substance. The next day, more garbage comes in and the BOMAGs add more soil. Operators retire, or close, landfills when they can't fit in any more garbage.

leachate collection tanks

ongoing unloading of garbage

methane wells/collection pipes

garbage-filled layers

leachate collection pipes

soil

methane-fueled electrical generation facility

gravel

geotextile mat

polyethylene liner

compacted clay

groundwater

SANITARY LANDFILL CROSS-SECTION

Sanitary landfills vary in size and depth. But most have a thick clay lining on the bottom and sides, several layers of absorbent substances on the bottom, and pipes for transporting liquid to the surface. Some landfills include pipes that collect methane for power generation.

As the garbage piles up in layers, it begins to rot under the layers of soil. Garbage contains many moist materials, such as wet scraps of food, discarded body lotions and cleaning solutions, leaky batteries, wet leaves, and soggy disposable diapers. Rain and snow seep through the layers of dirt, adding more moisture to the mix. The mass of wet, rotting garbage turns into a toxic leachate, which percolates down through the layers of trash and soil to the bottom of the pit. When the liquid reaches the thick liner inside the landfill, a system of pipes and pumps carries it up to tanks or ponds on the surface. Different landfills have different systems for treating toxic leachate. Some landfills clean it on-site, and others send it

TOXIC PLAYGROUNDS

Private companies and local governments run landfills throughout the United States. The EPA estimates that about thirty-one hundred landfills operate across the nation. Landfills have a life span of thirty to sixty years, and about ten thousand US landfills have been retired. The EPA requires owners of retired landfills to cover the sites with at least 24 inches (61 cm) of dirt and to restore the area by planting grass and trees.

Communities sometimes build playgrounds, dog parks, golf courses, ball fields, and schools upon retired landfills and even old toxic waste dumps. Environmentalists caution that such sites might not be safe. Testing at many sites has revealed dangerous levels of dioxin, arsenic, and other toxic materials in the soil, as well as contaminated groundwater. And even retired landfills can continue to emit methane, which is highly flammable and can cause explosions. For this reason, some parks built on old landfills do not allow smoking, grilling, and other activities that involve open flames.

Many parents are alarmed to learn that schools and children's play areas sit upon old landfills or hazardous waste dumps. In the first decade of the twenty-first century, concerned parents in Hamden, Connecticut, met with school officials after discovering that a middle school sat on the site of a long-abandoned industrial landfill. "We believe every day the children and staff have to continue at that school they are in danger," said one mother at the meeting. She continued, "We need to get everyone out of that building as soon as possible." Despite such concerns, the school remained open for several years before state environmental officials closed it and authorized cleanup at the site.

to city water treatment plants for cleaning. Cleaning the leachate separates the toxins from the water. The removed toxins become a sludge, which might be reburied in a landfill or pumped into a deep underground well. Workers purify the remaining water through chemical treatments and then discharge it into waterways.

THE TROUBLE WITH LANDFILLS

Even the most advanced construction techniques cannot keep landfills from leaking. Sharp objects in the trash can puncture landfill liners, and chemicals in the trash can corrode liners, allowing liquid to leak out. Landfill leakage also occurs when leachate drainage pipes clog or when drainage pumps break. An EPA survey of active landfills showed that 82 percent of liners were leaking to some degree. Leachate is highly toxic and pollutes land, groundwater, and waterways when it leaks. As the EPA explains, "Even the best liner and leachate collection system will ultimately fail due to natural deterioration . . . [although] releases may be delayed by many decades at some landfills."

This image shows leachate pumped from the bottom of a landfill draining into a leachate pond at the surface. The pond also holds stray pieces of garbage from the landfill. The company that operates the landfill will send the leachate to a water purification facility. Once the toxins are completely removed from the water, the cleaned water will drain into a river.

Leaking is not the only environmental hazard of landfills. They also contribute to climate change. Global temperatures have been rising steadily since 1955, and 2016 was the warmest year since scientists began keeping weather records in 1880. Warming temperatures are melting ice sheets in polar regions, and as meltwater drains into oceans, sea levels are rising. Increased air and water temperatures are also changing weather patterns on Earth, leading to extreme weather such as droughts, floods, wildfires, and hurricanes.

According to a 2014 report by the United Nations Intergovernmental Panel on Climate Change, rising temperatures are almost certainly anthropogenic, or caused by human activities. Humans are adding extra carbon dioxide, methane, and nitrous oxide into Earth's atmosphere. Called greenhouse gases, these gases trap the sun's heat near Earth in the same way that the glass roof of a greenhouse holds in heat to warm the plants inside. The burning of fossil fuels (oil, coal, and natural gas) to run cars, heat homes, power factories, and generate electricity releases carbon dioxide into the air. Deforestation also contributes to climate change. Plants take in carbon dioxide from the atmosphere and release oxygen. They use the carbon dioxide, along with sunlight and water, to make food. But when workers cut down or burn large areas of forest to make room for homes, farms, factories, or landfills, fewer trees are left to take in carbon dioxide.

Methane has twenty-five times the heat-trapping power of carbon dioxide, so it is a major contributor to climate change. The EPA states that methane is more abundant in the atmosphere than at any time in the past four hundred thousand years. In 2011 the atmosphere contained 150 percent more methane than it did in 1750. One reason for this increase is garbage. Methane forms when bacteria consume food scraps, animal manure, and other organic material (substances derived from living organisms). Decomposing garbage at landfills accounts for 18 percent of all anthropogenic methane production.

LANDFILL TO ENERGY

To reduce methane emissions at landfills, in 1994 the EPA started the Landfill Methane Outreach Program. In this program, landfill operators

NO LAUGHING MATTER

Livestock such as cattle, pigs, chickens, sheep, and goats account for 35 percent of all methane emissions worldwide. A single cow expels 26 to 53 gallons (98 to 200 liters) of methane every day when it burps and passes gas. While we tend to laugh when discussing cow flatulence, scientists say it is a major contributor to climate change. Beef, cow's milk, and other dairy products make up a large portion of the human diet, especially in the United States. Earth is home to more than 1.3 billion cows, with 100 million in the United States alone. The numbers add up to tens of billions of gallons of methane from cows each day.

Scientists are experimenting with several methods designed to rein in cow methane. Some researchers want to add enzymes and chemicals that block the production of methane to animal feed. Others are putting their faith in genetics. They want to selectively breed cows whose bodies naturally produce reduced levels of methane.

use extraction wells to pull methane from piles of rotting garbage. The wells are similar to those used to extract natural gas or oil from the ground. Drilling rigs dig boreholes into the garbage inside a landfill. Pipes fitted into the holes allow the methane to rise into collection and storage tanks. Energy companies buy the methane to make biogas, which is chemically similar to natural gas. People can burn biogas to power vehicles, generate heat for buildings, and create electricity for homes and businesses.

One of the largest landfill biogas producers in the world is the Puente Hills Landfill in the town of Whittier, about 12 miles (19 km) southeast of Los Angeles. This landfill is a towering trash monument to California consumerism. It started out as a regular garbage dump in the early 1950s. In 1983 it became the dumping ground for about one-half of all trash generated in Los Angeles County. In the twenty-first century, the landfill is known as Garbage Mountain, a pile of rubbish 500 feet (152 m) high, covering 700 acres (283 hectares) of land. The Puente Hills Landfill closed in November 2013, but the garbage there continues to emit methane. The

This aerial view of the Puente Hills Landfill, also known as Garbage Mountain, shows the scope of the landfill. Measuring 500 feet (152 m) in height, the landfill no longer receives trash, but the garbage continues to emit methane gas. Los Angeles County burns the gas to generate electricity.

county uses the gas to produce 50 megawatts of electricity daily, enough to power seventy thousand homes. Garbage Mountain is expected to continue producing methane until at least 2030.

The Landfill Methane Outreach Program is voluntary—landfills are not required to participate. Of the 3,100 landfills operating in the United States, only around 650 participate. Still, the program has helped reduce landfill methane emissions by 30 percent since the early 1990s. In 2015 the methane collected at landfills produced enough electricity to power about 1.3 million homes. But critics point out that even if the number of landfill-to-energy facilities were doubled, they would capture only about one-third of all methane produced by US landfills.

RECOVERING MATERIALS, REDUCING WASTE

When Puente Hills closed in 2013, it signaled a new direction for the management of household trash. Instead of sending half of the 7,500 tons (6,803 metric tons) of daily waste generated by its ten million residents to a landfill, Los Angeles County began sending it to materials recovery facilities (MRFs).

MRFs use new technology to separate reusable materials from trash before it goes to a landfill. Essentially, they sort out recyclable materials that ended up in trash bins instead of in recycling bins.

Los Angeles County sends some of its garbage to an MRF run by Athens Services, a private company. The Athens plant, which opened in 2014, is a state-of-the-art facility in Sun Valley, California. The plant is powered by rooftop solar panels. An odor-control system sprays chemicals throughout the facility to neutralize the smell of garbage. Inside the MRF, tons of garbage roll down the plant's conveyor belts past high-tech optical scanners. The scanners identify reusable materials in the trash, and automatically separates the materials into various categories for further handling. The categories are cardboard, newspaper, copper, aluminum, steel, glass, circuit boards, food, and several types of plastic. "What we do every morning is we wake up and try to find out how not to take things to a landfill," says Gary Clifford, executive vice president of Athens.

Once material has been sorted, it can be recycled. Paper and cardboard from the Athens facility goes to paper mills to be repurposed into new paper products. Glass, cans, and plastic are melted down and also recycled into new containers and other products. Food and garden waste is composted, or allowed to decay naturally. As it rots, it turns into a rich soil that farmers, gardeners, and park staff can use to fertilize trees and other plants. MRFs are a benefit for the environment, but they do have a downside: they are more expensive to operate than landfills. Many local governments can't afford MRFs so they continue to use landfills and garbage incinerators to handle massive amounts of trash.

BURNING GARBAGE

Incinerators provide an alternative to recycling or burying garbage, but they are the least used method for disposal. In the United States, only about 12 percent of trash is burned in incinerators.

Many modern garbage incinerators don't just burn trash. They also generate electricity. At these facilities, called energy-from-waste (EfW) systems, trash enters a combustion chamber, where it burns at 1,700°F (927°C). The heat from the incineration boils water stored in the system to create steam. The steam spins giant mechanical turbines to generate electricity, which provides power for homes and businesses.

As the garbage burns, filters within the EfW trap ash along with any metals and other materials that don't burn completely. Construction

Energy-from-waste (EfW) facilities, such as this one near Billingham in England, burn garbage to generate electric power. Filters trap some but not all of the toxins emitted from EfW smokestacks.

companies might use this material to make aggregate, or coarse particles similar to sand and crushed gravel. Aggregate is an ingredient in concrete and asphalt.

In 2015 eighty-six EfWs in the United States were together producing enough energy to power two million homes. And for every 1 ton (0.9 metric ton) of processed EfW garbage, about 1 ton of methane and carbon dioxide is not released into the atmosphere from a landfill.

Despite the benefits, many environmentalists oppose EfWs. Although they are less polluting than garbage burners of the twentieth century, the facilities still emit toxins through their smokestacks. Burning waste generates pollutants such as carbon monoxide, nitrogen oxides, lead, and mercury. Scrubbing devices in EfW smokestacks filter out most but not all of these pollutants. Some—such as mercury and lead—enter the atmosphere and can sicken humans and wildlife.

CHAPTER 3

TOXINS IN OUR TRASH

State of Emergency Following Massive Toxic Spill." "Environmental Agency Uncorks Its Own Toxic Water at Colorado Mine." These were some of the web and print headlines in August 2015 when a toxic waste disaster made international news.

In Silverton, Colorado, contractors working for the EPA were studying the abandoned Gold King Mine, located on a steep cliff above the Animas River. During the study, a worker operating a bulldozer accidentally broke through a dam made of rocks. It had been holding back 3 million gallons (11 million liters) of highly acidic wastewater, left behind by earlier mining operations. The water contained hazardous chemicals, including aluminum, cadmium, arsenic, and zinc. As the

Chemical-laden wastewater from mining operations, released by accident in 2015, turned Colorado's Animas River bright orange.

poisonous wastewater cascaded into the Animas, the crystal-clear river turned bright orange. Coloradans were shocked. "People think about Colorado for our skies and our landscapes and our rushing rivers," said John Hickenlooper, the state governor. "They don't want rivers to be orange."

The toxic waste quickly flowed downstream more than 100 miles (161 km) and from there into other rivers in Colorado, Utah, and New Mexico. Several days after the spill, hydrologists (scientists who study water) said that the mishap would not be easily fixed. The toxic plume settled onto river bottoms, where it will endanger downstream drinking water supplies for years to come. According to hydrologist Tom Myers, "There will be a source of these contaminants in the rivers for a long time. Every time there's a high flow [of water in the rivers] it will stir it up and it will be moving those contaminants downstream."

The Gold King is one of about 230 abandoned mines in Colorado and one of an estimated 500,000 abandoned mines in the United States. Many of these neglected diggings, known as hard rock mines, threaten water supplies. Hard rock mines are the source of valuable metals such as silver, gold, and copper, used to make thousands of consumer goods. When hard rock miners extract metals from the ground, they also dig up natural poisons in the soil, such as sulfur, arsenic, cadmium, lead, and mercury. Even tiny amounts of these substances can be deadly to humans and wildlife.

The EPA has regulations for the proper disposal of mine tailings (waste residue), but even so, toxins often contaminate air and water during mining operations. And the EPA rules were put in place long after the Gold King Mine was abandoned. That's why the toxic wastewater was still sitting at the site.

According to the EPA, hard rock mining releases 105 million pounds (48 million kg) of arsenic, 369 million pounds (167 million kg) of lead, and 4 million pounds (1.8 million kg) of mercury into the environment annually. In the western United States alone, these toxins contaminate 40 percent of all watersheds (areas drained by river systems). And sulfuric acid, a coal mining waste product, has permanently polluted thousands of miles of US watersheds.

Many other nations face similar dangers from mining. For example, China is the world's largest producer of gold. The country's gold mining industry produces 5.1 tons (4.6 metric tons) of cyanide for every 22 pounds (10 kg) of gold extracted from the ground.

COMPLEX CHEMICALS

While hard rock mining produces a significant amount of toxic waste, the chemical industry produces even more. Around 170 major chemical

WHAT IS HAZARDOUS WASTE?

The EPA has identified more than 650 hazardous chemicals commonly used in manufacturing. They fit into four broad categories: ignitable (can easily catch fire), corrosive (eats away at material), reactive (explodes or produces toxic gases), and toxic (poisonous).

- **Ignitable** chemicals create fires at very low temperatures—less than 140°F (60°C). Common ignitable substances include paint thinners, degreasers, and other industrial solvents.
- **Corrosive** chemicals can dissolve materials, including steel. Such chemicals include lye, rust removers, sulfuric acid, hydrochloric acid, battery acid, and some cleaning fluids. Waste that contains these chemicals is difficult to manage because, over time, corrosives destroy the waste containers they are stored in, allowing toxic materials to leak out.
- **Reactive** chemicals react when heated, compressed, or mixed with water or other materials. Waste containing reactive chemicals may create explosions or produce toxic gases. For example, lithium, found inside batteries in modern electronics, bursts into flames if mixed with water.
- **Toxic** substances can cause serious illness or death when swallowed or absorbed through the skin. Chemicals classified as toxic by the EPA include pesticides, cyanide, and chlorine.

companies operate in the United States. Many of them also operate internationally, with more than 2,800 facilities throughout the world.

These companies, including Dow Chemical, BASF, DuPont, ExxonMobil, and Monsanto, manufacture products such as dyes, detergents, insecticides, herbicides, and plastics. Often the manufacturing of these materials creates poisonous by-products. Each year American chemical companies produce about 265 million tons (240 metric tons) of toxic waste—1,700 pounds (771 kilograms) for every man, woman, and child in the United States. Worldwide, industry produces more than 400 million tons (363 million metric tons) of hazardous waste each year. In the twenty-first century, most US-based companies dispose of their waste

Around the world, including the United States, many farmers spray herbicides to destroy weeds growing in their fields, and they spray pesticides to kill bugs that prey on crops. Many of these chemicals are listed on the EPA's Toxics Release Inventory. Heavy rains often wash the toxins into nearby waterways, where they can poison wildlife.

according to EPA regulations. But the largest chemical companies have been in operation since the early twentieth century, and for decades, they dumped pollution with little regard for the environment.

The EPA lists more than 650 hazardous chemicals and tracks their production and disposal on a list called the Toxics Release Inventory (TRI). Every chemical on the TRI can create health problems in humans and animals, ranging from minor issues such as skin irritation to deadly ones such as cancer. Most Americans have little knowledge about these hazardous toxins, but some of them have gained widespread notoriety.

DOW AND DIOXIN

Dioxin—a family of seventy-five compounds, each with a similar chemical structure—is one of the deadliest chemicals on the TRI. It is a by-product of several manufacturing processes. For instance, bleaching paper, burning industrial waste, and manufacturing plastics and pesticides all form dioxin.

The EPA labels dioxin as a carcinogen (cancer-causing agent). It is also linked to diabetes, learning disabilities, lung problems, and skin disorders. Dioxin commonly enters the human body through food. The process begins when industry illegally dumps dioxin into waterways or legally burns it in incinerators. The smoke from incinerators contains trace amounts of dioxin, which then settles back onto land or water. In waterways, fish can inadvertently ingest dioxin with their food. Livestock ingest dioxin that lands on fields where they graze or crops used to make animal feed. Tiny amounts of the chemical then enter the bodies of humans who eat the fish or meat. Over time, dioxin levels in the body add up and can lead to health problems.

Dioxin is an endocrine disrupter. The human endocrine system is a collection of glands that release hormones into the blood. Hormones regulate growth, reproduction, and many other biological functions. Dioxin disrupts the natural hormonal balance in the human body by mimicking the hormone estrogen. The body thinks it has too much of the hormone, and the disruption can cause tumors in the breast, uterus, or prostate. Endocrine disrupters can also increase the risk of birth defects, disrupt normal sexual development, and decrease fertility (the ability to reproduce). When endocrine disrupters pollute waterways, the chemicals can alter the balance of sex hormones in fish, disrupting their reproductive abilities.

One of the worst dioxin hot spots in the world is the Tittabawassee River. It flows past the headquarters of the Dow Chemical Company in Midland, Michigan. Since its founding in 1897, Dow has manufactured more than one thousand chemicals that produce dioxin as a by-product. Before the EPA created regulations to govern the handling of industrial waste, Dow dumped the chemicals directly into the river and burned them in industrial incinerators. The Tittabawassee River has the highest levels of dioxin contamination ever measured in the United States. It drains into the Saginaw River and eventually flows into Lake Huron, a Great Lake that

For many decades in the twentieth century, Dow Chemical dumped cancer-causing dioxin into the Tittabawassee River in central Michigan. The EPA ordered Dow to clean up the river, but the company fought back in court. The EPA finally won the lawsuit, and Dow began cleanup efforts in 2011.

provides drinking water for 1.5 million area residents. In the late 1980s, the EPA tried to hold Dow accountable for its dioxin pollution and required the company to clean up the toxic waste. However, for decades Dow fought the EPA order in court. Finally, in 2011 the EPA prevailed, and Dow began removing contaminated sediment from the Tittabawassee and burying it in landfills. The company plans to have the entire watershed cleaned by 2021. Meanwhile, a 2011 study showed that women living in Midland and counties downstream from Dow Chemical have significantly higher rates of breast cancer than those in the rest of the United States, and health officials believe that dioxin is to blame.

TOXIC HYDROCARBONS

Numerous industrial chemicals are made from compounds called hydrocarbons. As the name implies, hydrocarbons combine hydrogen and carbon. Petroleum—the source of many fuels and plastics—contains many hydrocarbons.

Manufacturers use the hydrocarbon benzene to produce drugs, dyes, detergents, insecticides, plastics, and synthetic rubber. Some products naturally contain benzene. For instance, benzene exists in crude oil, from which we get gasoline. Even after processing, every gallon (4 liters) of car fuel is about 2 percent benzene. The EPA classifies benzene as a carcinogen. It is also classed as a teratogen, a product that can cause deformities in human fetuses. Scientists believe that humans take benzene into their bodies when they breathe gasoline fumes at gas stations and breathe motor vehicle exhaust along roadways. Benzene (and other hydrocarbon) pollution is particularly severe in many nations of the Middle East. This region has vast petroleum deposits and a booming petroleum industry but few environmental regulations to protect air, soil, and waterways.

Chemicals called halogenated hydrocarbons are also highly poisonous. One of the deadliest forms of halogenated hydrocarbon is the chemical trichlorophenol (TCP), commonly used in herbicides (weed killers). Industry once viewed halogenated hydrocarbons called polychlorinated biphenyls (PCBs) as miracle chemicals. PCBs are extremely heat resistant and will not catch fire when exposed to electricity. So PCB-based oil was ideal insulation for transformers that convert high-voltage electricity from power plants into safer, low-voltage electricity for households. Builders installed millions of transformers filled with PCB oil atop utility poles and in residential and commercial buildings. Manufacturers also used PCBs to make hydraulic fluids (for engines, car brakes, and other machines), sealants, caulking, synthetic rubber, paint, and asphalt. Between 1930 and 1977, Monsanto manufactured all the PCBs.

For nearly fifty years, companies that bought PCBs from Monsanto handled the chemical carelessly. It made its way into sewers, streams, and landfills through spills, leaks, and improper storage. One of the biggest PCB polluters was General Electric (GE). While making heavy-duty electrical equipment, GE discharged 1.3 million pounds (0.6 million kg) of PCBs into the Hudson River near its plant in Hudson Falls, New York. It discharged another 1.6 million pounds (0.7 million kg) of PCBs into an underground reservoir beneath a company parking lot.

Scientific studies have linked PCBs to birth defects, cancer, liver damage, and other serious health problems in humans. It is also extremely toxic to marine animals such as porpoises, whales, and various seabirds. Company records show that Monsanto recognized the toxic properties of PCBs as early as 1937. But it wasn't until 1977, after the US government announced that it would ban the chemicals, that Monsanto ceased production of PCBs. While Monsanto has not manufactured PCBs for decades, they remain in the environment because they take centuries to break down. PCBs contaminate nearly every waterway in the world—from the Southern Ocean around Antarctica to the Bering Sea between Russia and Alaska.

THE TOXIC TRAIL OF CONSUMER GOODS

Manufacturing consumer goods can also generate toxic by-products. For example, Americans annually spend more than $52 billion on products such as bleach, laundry soap, cleanser, and toilet bowl cleaner.

Producing many of these goods generates toxins such as mercury, chlorine, and asbestos.

Even toothpaste is part of the toxic waste problem. Many consumers want their toothpaste to be sparkling white—perhaps believing that bright white toothpaste equates with bright white teeth. To satisfy this demand, manufacturers use an agent called super white titanium dioxide. Companies also use it to whiten paper and some foods. The leading manufacturer of super white titanium dioxide is the Chemours Company (owned by DuPont until 2015), which makes the substance in DeLisle, Mississippi. Every year, while producing super white titanium dioxide, the plant creates more than 12 million pounds (5.4 million kg) of hazardous waste by-products, including dioxin, chromium, and nickel. Since the plant opened in 1979, it has carelessly released such toxins into the air, the groundwater, and waterways along the coast of the Gulf of Mexico.

Some brands of air freshener, nail polish, and perfume contain chemicals called phthalates. Phthalates make nail polish spread more easily onto fingernails and toenails and help air fresheners and perfumes spray more evenly. But like dioxin, phthalates are endocrine disrupters, linked to reproductive problems and birth defects. Cosmetics contain other toxic chemicals. For instance, some kinds of mascara contain mercury, and certain brands of lipstick contain lead and arsenic.

Toxins are common in plastics too. Polyethylene terephthalate (PET) is used to make trillions of bottles to hold water and other beverages. Toxins contained in PET include nickel, ethyl oxide, acetone, and benzene. These chemicals can migrate from a plastic bottle to the beverage it contains. Drinking the beverage brings the toxins into a person's body. PET is carcinogenic and can cause birth defects, endocrine disruption, and other negative health impacts.

Another type of harmful plastic, polyvinyl chloride (PVC), is found in food packaging, plastic food wrap, food containers, shower curtains, garden hoses, and thousands of other consumer products. Nearly 50 percent of toys sold in the United States, including bath toys, dolls, and Halloween

NASTY NUCLEAR WASTE

In 2016 thirty-one countries across the globe used nuclear power plants to generate electricity. In the United States, nearly 20 percent of all electricity comes from nuclear power. France gets more than three-quarters of its electricity from nuclear power, while Belgium, Sweden, and South Korea rely on nuclear power plants for about one-third of their electricity.

While nuclear power does not directly contribute to climate change, the waste created by the world's 444 nuclear power plants is a problem that will not go away. The waste from nuclear power will remain highly toxic to people, animals, and the environment for 240,000 years.

Nuclear power plants use uranium pellets packed inside metal rods to boil water, creating steam that spins turbines and generates electricity. Uranium is radioactive—it gives off highly dangerous radiation. It remains radioactive after it is used as fuel.

Around the world, an estimated 275,000 tons (250,000 metric tons) of spent uranium waste is in storage, most of it in thick concrete casks kept at nuclear power facilities. Dry cask storage is a temporary solution because the radioactive waste will eventually corrode the casks, causing them to leak.

Scientists say that the only way to safely dispose of nuclear waste is to bury it deep underground. But no country on Earth has created a safe storage site for nuclear waste. The US government began work in 2002 to construct a disposal site called the Yucca Mountain Nuclear Waste Repository in Nevada. But fear of accidents and earthquakes that might release the waste into the environment, as well as resistance from local residents, have delayed the project. It is uncertain when and if it will open.

costumes, as well as kids' backpacks and lunch boxes, are made of PVC. Scientists consider PVC to be one of the most toxic types of plastic for several reasons. Not only does its production release dioxins into the atmosphere, but it also contains phthalates and flame-retardants, which make it fire resistant. By touching products that contain PVCs or by eating and drinking from containers made with PVCs, consumers can absorb the toxins through their skin, ingest them by mouth, or breathe in their fumes.

Thousands of products that consumers use every day, including school backpacks, are made from PVC, a toxic type of plastic. These students are in New York City.

Adverse health effects associated with PVCs include cancer, birth defects, skin diseases, bronchitis, and liver problems.

PUMPING WASTE UNDERGROUND

Releasing toxins into the air and dumping toxic chemicals into waterways and landfills is not safe for humans, animals, or plants. But for decades, it was not prohibited in the United States or any other country. By the 1970s, the EPA had set rules and regulations for the safer disposal of toxic waste in the United States, and many other nations followed suit. Companies that ignored the rules faced lawsuits, heavy fines, and court-ordered mandates to clean up their pollution. Yet in the twenty-first century, the safe disposal of toxic chemicals is still a pressing problem because the accepted methods for handling hazardous waste are not 100 percent safe.

For example, to legally dispose of toxic waste from manufacturing and oil drilling, the EPA recommends a method called deep-well injection (DWI). In DWI, workers pump hazardous liquids into metal and concrete pipes sunk deep into the ground. The waste flows into natural caves or between layers of rock as low as 2 miles (3.2 km) underground. Engineers try to deposit waste between layers of impermeable rock, with no faults or cracks through which the waste can leak out. Well bottoms are also far below any area aquifers (natural underground pools of water from which humans draw their water supplies).

More than 680,000 injection wells operate in the United States. Since the early 1990s, industry has pumped more than 30 trillion gallons (114 trillion liters) of toxic liquid into these wells. The liquid includes poisonous waste from manufacturing and mining, toxic sludge from landfill leachate, and chemical-laden wastewater from an oil and natural gas extraction process called fracking.

DWI began in the United States in the late twentieth century. At first, the EPA set extremely strict rules for DWI operations. Companies had to design wells that would not leak and threaten underground water supplies for at least ten thousand years. But the multibillion-dollar oil and gas industry pushed back hard, saying that the rules were too strict and too expensive to comply with. The industry's successful lobbying has led to looser restrictions for the disposal of toxic waste from fracking and other oil and gas operations. In the twenty-first century, the strictest DWI regulations are reserved only for the most hazardous waste, such as PCBs, TCPs, and other deadly compounds.

In 2012 investigative journalist Abrahm Lustgarten researched DWIs in the United States and uncovered some disturbing facts. In the online

FRACKING FOR OIL AND GAS

Oil and gas companies use fracking to extract natural gas and petroleum trapped deep underground in shale formations. Fracking involves blasting millions of gallons of water, sand, and chemicals into a well to fracture the shale. Oil and gas flow to the surface through the fractured rock, along with polluted wastewater. The water can contain up to 630 chemicals, some of them highly toxic, including hydrochloric acid, kerosene, diesel fuel, and toluene. According to a 2010 study by environmental health analyst Theo Colborn, 93 percent of the chemicals used in fracking can sicken people and animals.

newspaper *ProPublica*, he reported that between 2007 and 2010, inspectors found that the metal and concrete walls of more than seven thousand US injection wells were leaking. He stressed that geologists have noted waste leaking out of underground rock formations in unexpected ways and sometimes migrating into aquifers. In some cases, toxic waste has bubbled up to the surface and into public parks. Many states manage DWI systems poorly. They do not inspect DWI systems thoroughly, address leaking wells adequately, or issue harsh penalties to businesses that violate regulations.

While many scientists and government regulators acknowledge that pumping waste underground is a flawed system, they say that the alternatives to DWI are also problematic. These alternatives include burying waste in landfills and burning it in incinerators, both of which also pollute the air, soil, and water. The alternatives are also more expensive than DWI technology.

PROTECTING HUMAN HEALTH

Many Americans believe that government agencies test and regulate all consumer products to ensure that they are not toxic. But that's not the case. For instance, the US government does not tightly regulate the cosmetics industry. Cosmetics makers must list any color additives in their products but not other ingredients—even toxic chemicals. While some manufacturers are forthcoming about ingredients, others are not. In total, manufacturers and industries use about eighty-five thousand chemicals to make products, but the US government has tested only a fraction of them for safety. The EPA does not have enough money or personnel to study every new chemical that comes on the market. And manufacturers would make less money if they had to comply with stricter EPA regulations, so they fight any efforts to tighten regulations. Because of well-funded and effective industry lobbying, the EPA has banned only five substances since 1976.

Studies show that 92 percent of Americans have toxic chemicals from plastics in their bodies. Other studies reveal that our bodies contain toxins from paint, car exhaust, household cleaners, and other everyday items. The chemical industry argues that the amounts in our bodies are so tiny that they do not affect our health. Doctors, researchers, and other experts disagree. According to the National Institutes of Health, long-term exposure to even small amounts of chemicals like PVC and benzene pose serious health risks. Research also shows that the toxic effects of chemicals may be amplified as they interact with one another in the human body.

It's hard to protect yourself from chemical contaminants, since manufacturers aren't required to list them on product labels. But you can still do much to avoid dangerous toxins. Look for food products that are promoted as being pesticide- and herbicide-free. Purchase nail polish and other cosmetics made without toxic toluene, formaldehyde, and phthalates. At food co-ops and other natural food stores, purchase cleaning supplies made without toxic dyes, fragrances, and brighteners. Or create your own nontoxic cleaning supplies using natural substances such as vinegar and baking soda.

To limit exposure to plastic toxins, cut back on the amount of plastic you use every day. For example, experts recommend replacing plastic food containers with glass or ceramic ones. Wrap lunch foods in unbleached paper sandwich bags instead of plastic wrap. Choose a glass water bottle or a ceramic mug for beverages. Ask your parents to use cloth shower curtains instead of plastic ones. Wash your hands after handling plastics that contain PVCs.

Using nontoxic products can help keep you safer, but consumer advocates, public health experts, and environmentalists want to see the US government do more to protect citizens. They want the government to ban or strictly regulate each industrial chemical until tests show that it is safe for humans and the environment. US manufacturers strongly object to such measures because they would cost money to implement, slow down production, and cut into business profits. In the end, Americans have to decide which is more important—profits made by industry or the health and safety of consumers.

CHAPTER 4
TAKE CONTROL OF YOUR PLATE

The French popularized champagne, croissants, and four hundred distinct types of cheese. And in France, a two-hour lunch is not uncommon, especially on the weekends. It should come as no surprise, then, that France is also leading the war against food waste. In 2015 the French government passed a law that forbids supermarkets from throwing out unsold food. Large French restaurants must offer customers takeaway containers or "doggie bags." The French law says that supermarkets must donate any unsold but still edible food to charity for immediate distribution to the needy. They must donate food that is spoiling or otherwise

Around the world, about one-third of the food produced for human consumption ends up in landfills, is burned in incinerators, or sits in farm fields to rot. The discarded food comes from farms, food processors, grocery stores, restaurants, and households.

unsafe for human consumption to farmers, who will feed it to livestock or compost it for fertilizer. The French are very serious about not wasting food. Those who violate the law face up to $81,600 in fines or two years in prison.

The French law is the first on Earth to address a widespread crisis. In a world where millions of people are starving, up to one-third of the planet's food is wasted. Grocery stores in industrialized countries are among the major food wasters. They routinely throw away perfectly edible produce because it has slight blemishes. They reject produce, dairy products, and other items that are past the manufacturer's suggested "use-by" date but that are actually still safe to eat.

French lawmakers were driven to pass the unsold food law by grim statistics that the United Nations (UN) World Food Programme released in 2015. According to the international organization, one out of every nine humans on Earth faces starvation on a daily basis. That's 795 million people. Another 2 billion people are food-insecure: they are undernourished and often miss meals because food is not always available. About one-third of the food-insecure are children. According to the Feeding America food bank, even in the United States, the richest nation on Earth, about 48 million people are food-insecure. That's more than one in seven people.

While nearly half the population of Earth worry about where their next meal is coming from, consumers and businesses trash mountains of food every day. According to the UN's Food and Agriculture Organization (FAO), every year humans throw out about one-third of the food produced on Earth. In the United States, around 40 percent of the food supply goes uneaten every year, according to a 2014 United States Department of Agriculture (USDA) study. This translates into 133 billion pounds (60 billion kg) of food, worth about $165 billion, going to the dump annually. The amount of food wasted in the United States equals 20 pounds (9 kg) per person per month. That is almost 50 percent more food wasted than in 1990 and nearly three times what Americans discarded in 1960.

Millions of people on Earth don't have regular access to healthy food because of war, poverty, and environmental disaster. These children, for example, have fled war in Syria and are waiting in a food distribution line at a refugee camp in Turkey. But while they and millions of others around the globe are food-insecure, tons of food go to waste each year. If the United States and other wealthy nations were to donate food waste, everyone on Earth would have more than enough to eat.

The statistics on food waste are similar in other wealthy countries. Together, consumers in rich countries waste almost as much food as farmers in sub-Saharan Africa, the region south of the Sahara, produce each year. There, two hundred million people suffer from chronic hunger. German filmmaker and author Valentin Thurn puts the statistics in perspective: "The number of calories that end up in the garbage in North America and Europe would be sufficient to feed the hungry of this world three times over."

THE FOOD WASTE CHAIN

Food waste is defined as edible food that is available for human consumption but is not actually eaten. Uneaten food discarded after a meal is called plate waste. Discarded food is the single largest source of waste in US and European landfills, where the rotting fruits, veggies, and animal products not only go to waste, but they also generate methane, contributing to climate change.

Much food waste begins at home. In the United Kingdom, each household throws away about $350 worth of uneaten food every year. But as with most things concerning trash, the United States is number one. Every year, the average American household of four spends between $1,365 and $2,275 on food that ends up in the garbage can. Why do Americans throw away so much food? Often the family chef simply prepares more food than the family can eat, dishing out large portions, much of which ends up as plate waste. Similar waste occurs in restaurants, where diners leave about 17 percent of their food uneaten. Many fast-food restaurants are famous for their supersized portions, containing more food than most people can eat in one sitting. And restaurants must have extra food on hand to make everything on their menus—even dishes that are rarely ordered. Fast-food restaurants routinely prepare perfectly edible food that's never served. For example, McDonald's requires workers to trash french fries that are more than seven minutes old so that customers do not receive soggy fries.

A great amount of food waste in the United States and some other nations results from containers that bear "sell by," "use by," or "best before" labels, followed by dates. Contrary to popular belief, the dates are not

AN EATER'S MANUAL

Renowned food activist and journalist Michael Pollan has written numerous books about food. His 2009 book *Food Rules: An Eater's Manual* offers sixty-four tips about healthy eating. In 2014 Pollan created a new rule concerning food waste. In the excerpt below, he urges consumers to "take control of their plates":

> Supersized portions have become the bane of both our health and the health of the planet. Most of us eat what's put in front of us, ignoring signals of satiety [fullness]; the only possible outcomes are either overeating or food waste. Gluttony is never pretty, but when a billion people in the world are hungry, it becomes [unacceptable]. So if you're serving yourself, take no more than you know you can finish; err on the side of serving yourself too little, since you can always go back for seconds. When you're at a restaurant that serves [huge] portions, tell your server you'd prefer a modest serving and the option of asking for more if it doesn't satisfy. . . . We need a movement to make reasonable portions and "seconds" the norm in restaurants. That way, the restaurant can still offer the perceived value of "all you can eat" but without the inevitable waste.

related to food safety, and the US government does not regulate them. Manufacturers put the dates on products to show when the food is at its peak quality. Many consumers assume that food should not be eaten after the date listed and throw it out. But in fact, some foods are edible for days, weeks, or even months past a "use by" date. Nutritionists say that if food is spoiled, it will be obvious to the consumer. Spoiled bread, milk, cheese, meat, and other perishables appear moldy or emit noticeably nasty smells.

While homes, grocery stores, and restaurants account for great amounts of food loss, even more waste occurs before food ever gets to these places. Dana Gunders, lead scientist for the Natural Resources Defense Council (NRDC), explains that much food waste occurs on farms. The reasons are economic. Farmers may actually save money by leaving a certain percentage of their crops in their fields to rot. Gunders elaborates, "If market prices are too low at the time of harvest, growers may leave some crops in the

Depending on market fluctuations, farmers may actually spend more to raise and harvest food crops than they would earn by selling them. In these circumstances, a farmer may choose to let the food rot. At this banana plantation in Panama, for example, farmworkers have dumped bananas in a field rather than take them to market.

field because they will not cover their costs [of growing the crops] after accounting for the costs of labor [wages] and transport [shipping crops to warehouses and stores]." Feeding America, which runs more than two hundred food banks in the United States, says that US farmers leave 6 billion pounds (2.7 billion kg) of fresh produce to rot in their fields every year.

Even after harvesting crops, farmers might toss them because they don't look appealing to eat. US consumers have come to expect vegetables and fruits to look a certain way, and many shoppers won't buy produce that is misshapen or blemished. Knowing this, growers toss around 35 percent of edible potatoes because they are misshapen, contain small gray spots, or have small (but harmless) cavities at their centers.

Similarly, food processors frequently discard food that doesn't meet certain standards for size, color, and weight. The NRDC reports that workers at one large tomato-packing house in California fill a dump truck with 22,000 pounds (9,979 kg) of discarded tomatoes every forty minutes during harvest season. Another produce packer told the NRDC that 20 to 50 percent of the fruit that comes to his facility cannot be sold because of its appearance. While some of the rejected produce is canned for human consumption or is fed to animals, millions of tons end up in landfills.

Similar visual culling takes place at grocery stores. Food retailers in industrialized nations observe that customers are more likely to buy produce from a fully stocked display. They note that shoppers resist picking items from a small pile of oranges or broccoli, for example. To build the big piles and pyramids of produce that appeal to consumers, grocers buy more than they plan to sell. As shoppers pick the attractive fruits and vegetables from the top of the pile, the food at the bottom of the display often gets squashed and damaged. Grocery workers ultimately throw it away.

WASTING NATURAL RESOURCES

Wasted food is connected to the misuse of precious natural resources. In the United States, agriculture accounts for the use of 10 percent of energy, 50 percent of land, and 80 percent of freshwater. To grow food, farmers

use hundreds of millions of pounds of polluting fertilizers, pesticides, and herbicides. But 40 percent of the food won't ever be eaten. So Americans are using massive amounts of energy and water while adding toxic chemicals to the environment on an unprecedented scale only to throw away a large portion of that food.

According to the Consultative Group on International Agricultural Research, the global food system creates one-third of all global carbon emissions. Farm machinery, fertilizer plants, food refrigerators, and vehicles that transport food all run on fossil fuels and emit tons of carbon dioxide into the atmosphere. The livestock industry alone contributes 18 percent of global carbon emissions. A 2006 report by the FAO showed that beef production generates more carbon dioxide (and methane emissions) than the entire transportation sector worldwide. The situation makes food waste "an often overlooked aspect of climate change," says UN secretary-general Ban Ki-moon.

The food waste dilemma poses ethical questions as well. Even as livestock production is increasing climate change, US consumers continue to throw away large amounts of beef, pork, chicken, and turkey. According to a vegetarian blogger who goes by the name Harish, wasting all this meat is morally wrong. Harish notes that large industrial farms crowd food animals into dirty pens, stalls, and cages while they are being fattened up and readied for slaughter. "Even most [meat eaters] would agree that there is something deeply wretched about inflicting lifelong pain and misery and finally death on an animal for food we are *not* going to eat," writes Harish.

THE WOODSTOCK OF FOOD WASTE

Would you take a pledge not to waste food? Many residents of the British city of London are doing just that. Activists there founded a campaign called Feeding the 5000 in 2009 to draw public attention to food waste. The name comes from the organization's practice of feeding large crowds a free feast made from top-quality produce that otherwise would have been thrown away.

MEATLESS MONDAYS

Producing meat eats up vast amounts of precious resources, such as water and land, and a lot of the meat produced for food goes to waste. One solution: eat less meat! The organization Meatless Monday, based in Baltimore, Maryland, educates people on the health and environmental benefits of giving up meat for just one day a week.

Launched with the Johns Hopkins Bloomberg School of Public Health in 2003, Meatless Monday is active in thirty-six countries. The American Meat Institute estimated in 2011 that 18 percent of US households were participating in Meatless Monday. Programs such as Meatless Monday are among dozens worldwide aimed at reducing food waste and promoting good health. From the farm field to the dinner table, people are learning that slaughtering animals only to throw their meat into the garbage bin is bad for Earth and its inhabitants.

The first Feeding the 5000 event was in London's famous Trafalgar Square. There, organizers fed thousands of servings of curry, fruit smoothies, salads, and steamed vegetables to anyone who showed up. In following years, Feeding the 5000 held events in France, Ireland, the Netherlands, and Australia, and it continues to host feasts. The group encourages its guests to take a food waste pledge. They make a commitment to reduce food waste while asking businesses and governments to address the crisis.

Feeding the 5000 came to Oakland, California, in October 2014 as part of an event dubbed the Woodstock of Food Waste. While the original three-day Woodstock rock music festival attracted half a million attendees to upstate New York in 1969, the Woodstock of Food Waste involved four days of seminars, cooking events, and field trips to area farms. The event, hosted by EndFoodWaste.org, attracted food waste experts from sixteen states and seven countries, as well as filmmakers, government representatives, food researchers, grocers, restaurant owners, consumers, and students.

The finale of the Woodstock of Food Waste was a free Feeding the 5000 meal in Oakland. Hundreds of volunteers peeled, chopped, and

SPREADING THE MESSAGE

In September 2015, dozens of world leaders gathered for a lunch at UN headquarters in New York City. UN secretary-general Ban Ki-moon had called together the high-powered officials to discuss important issues concerning climate change. Ban wanted to make a point about food waste and climate change, so he hired former White House chef Sam Kass and prominent New York chef Dan Barber to create the entire lunch from food that would otherwise have been thrown away.

Kass and Barber fed the attendees vegetable burgers made from pulp left over from juicing vegetables. The french fries were created from cornstarch, a by-product of corn. Other ingredients included grain left over from brewing beers, blemished produce that would not normally be displayed in a store, and vegetable scraps such as stalks and leaves that usually end up in the garbage can. Barber said he hoped to inspire world leaders to think about the impact that food waste has on the climate. "You don't do that by lecturing, you do it [by] making these world leaders have a delicious meal that will make them think about spreading that message."

cooked food that was not appealing enough to sell at grocery stores and fed it to about two thousand diners that day. The feast included more than four thousand day-old loaves of bread and rolls rescued from local bakeries. In addition, volunteers cooked soup for three thousand meals and froze it for later distribution at local soup kitchens. Amy Leibrock, a blogger for the environmental organization Sustainable America, wrote about the Oakland feast:

> The event saved 11,200 pounds [5,080 kg] of apples, sweet potatoes, carrots, onions, acorn squash and spaghetti squash that normally would have been destroyed because they were cosmetically imperfect and could not be sold to grocery stores. This included onions that were "too big" and carrots that were "too long and skinny." I ate a couple of the rescued apples—they were both crisp and juicy with a few dark spots on the skin. They were more than just edible—they were delicious.

Volunteers with Feeding the 5000 hand out free meals in Union Square Park in New York City in May 2015. The meals consist of food that would otherwise have been thrown away. After launching in London in 2000, Feeding the 5000 is taking its program around the world.

After the success in Oakland, Feeding the 5000 expanded its program to include other US cities, including New York City; Washington, DC; and Omaha, Nebraska. The events attracted a great deal of public attention to issues surrounding food waste. According to Feeding the 5000 organizer Jordan Figueiredo, "This problem, what I believe is *the* [social and] environmental challenge of our time, is actually the socio-environmental opportunity of our time as well, and a movement is building in the [United States] to seize this opportunity to end food waste and hunger."

UGLY PRODUCE

Young adults are finding creative ways to save "ugly" fruits and vegetables. In May 2014, University of Maryland student Evan Lutz founded a charitable business called Hungry Harvest. His goal was to make ugly fruits and vegetables beautiful to consumers. Hungry Harvest operates in Baltimore, Maryland; Washington, DC; and Philadelphia, Pennsylvania. Its workers gather visually imperfect produce from farmers and food sellers

within a 200-mile (322 km) radius of each city. Subscribers sign up with Hungry Harvest for weekly or biweekly delivery of about 6 pounds (2.7 kg) of recovered produce. Prices are about 30 percent lower than those in local grocery stores. For every bag of produce Hungry Harvest delivers to its customers, the company donates 2 pounds (0.9 kg) of produce to food banks. By May 2016, the organization had rescued a total of 500,000 pounds (226,796 kg) of produce. Of that food, the company donated about 185,000 pounds (83,914 kg) of produce to food banks and soup kitchens.

Lutz appeared on the ABC reality show *Shark Tank* in 2016 to ask the show's panel of investors to provide money to help his company grow. *Shark Tank* investor Robert Herjavec wrote Hungry Harvest a $100,000 check in exchange for 10 percent of the business. After that show, the number of Hungry Harvest customers doubled from six hundred to twelve hundred. Lutz plans to begin operations in New York City in 2017.

APP-ETIZING

Zero Percent, founded by Pakistan native Raj Karmani in 2012, uses technology to tackle food waste. Karmani obtained a PhD in computer science at the University of Illinois in Urbana-Champaign and decided to use his education for social good rather than personal enrichment. After seeing a manager of a Chicago bagel shop throw away dozens of perfectly good bagels at the end of the day, Karmani looked into food waste and invented the Zero Percent app. It connects Chicago restaurants and food sellers with charities that distribute food to the hungry. Food pantries using the app receive text alerts about which businesses have leftover food and then send trucks to pick it up.

In less than two years after its founding, Zero Percent delivered 903,000 meals to hungry Chicago citizens. But the system had a problem. Many of the businesses donating food were in downtown Chicago while the charities were 15 to 20 miles (24 to 32 km) away in South and West Chicago. The transportation costs were higher than the value of the donated food. The charities couldn't afford to send trucks to get the food.

To cover the transportation costs, Karmani launched the crowdfunding website www.foodrescue.io, which encourages visitors to donate to Zero Percent. Karmani says that a five-dollar donation can provide fifteen meals for those in need while keeping 18 pounds (8 kg) of food out of landfills.

INFORMATION IS THE KEY

The USDA has pledged to reduce food waste in the United States by 50 percent before 2030. Achieving that objective might be difficult, as shown by a 2014 consumer poll taken by the packaging company Sealed Air. According to the poll, 63 percent of respondents were concerned about the amount of food wasted in the United States. However, only 34 percent were worried about the food they wasted in their own homes. So two-thirds of those polled believed food waste was someone else's problem. In a nation where consumers throw out more than one-third of the food they buy, they seem to have a great deal of denial about who is throwing away all that food.

The Sealed Air poll provided some encouraging news, however. When respondents learned about the environmental, economic, and social impacts of food waste, 59 percent said the impacts were greater than they expected. After hearing the facts, 73 percent said they would make it a higher priority to limit food waste in their homes, proving that information is the key to solving the problem.

Those involved with the issue of food waste, from food activists to the United Nations, believe it is possible to massively reduce the amount of food going into the trash. It will be a global effort. In 2015 the United Nations set a goal of reducing world food waste by half by 2030. Doing so will require both changes in food production and distribution and increased public awareness. As with other garbage problems, the solutions to food waste are within the grasp of each individual. In fact, if everyone on Earth pledged to toss less food, many problems associated with food waste could be solved in a matter of months.

CHAPTER 5

A GRAVEYARD OF GLOBAL WASTE

magine townspeople not only living *with* garbage but practically living *in* garbage. That's what US author Roma Eisenstark saw when she traveled to China in 2015 to work as an English teacher in a small rural village in China's Hebei Province. The village is a three-hour drive from Beijing, China's capital, and is surrounded by farm fields, rivers, marshes, and lakes. But it is also practically submerged in garbage. According to Eisenstark, the town's roadsides, riverbanks, and lakeshores are littered with "heaps of plastic cups, candy wrappers, napkins, and an endless multitude of plastic bags . . . in every possible size, shape, and color . . . old sandals, hairbrushes, broken children's toys, sweaters."

Workers clean up trash along the bank of the Yangtze River in the Chinese city of Yichang. Many Chinese towns have no landfills or incinerators to handle their garbage, so residents simply dump it outdoors.

Eisenstark soon discovered that the town, like thousands of other Chinese villages, has changed rapidly in recent decades. Until the 1990s, rural residents in China produced and owned few consumer goods and therefore produced little garbage. They did not need large-scale waste management systems. However, in 2014 China overtook the United States as the world's largest economy. Every year, it produces more than $2 trillion in consumer goods. The nation produces almost all the world's electronic devices and about half of all other global retail products. Factories have opened in rural towns and villages across China, providing jobs for millions and boosting the nation's economy. The rapid economic growth has brought prosperity to China, but it has also resulted in an explosion of garbage and toxic waste. Governments in rural China do not have the money to build landfills, garbage incinerators, or other trash facilities to handle the garbage. In the town where Eisenstark lived, discarded packaging litters the countryside and harms the environment. A local lake, once famous for its beauty, is barren. The fish and other aquatic creatures that once lived there have been poisoned by toxic chemicals and by ingesting tiny pieces of plastic, which the animals mistook for food. Near the school where Eisenstark worked, maintenance workers burn garbage in open pits, polluting the air with deadly toxins.

AN ARMY OF RECYCLERS

While living in rural China, Eisenstark traveled to Beijing every week. She began packing her garbage to dispose of it safely there. With an estimated metropolitan population of 24.9 million, Beijing has organized public sanitation. The city's ten thousand garbage trucks collect trash every day and dump it at a number of city-run landfills and incinerators. However, Beijing does not operate a citywide recycling service. City residents mix all their food waste, packaging, and recyclable materials in the trash.

Instead of city-run recycling, an army of around two hundred thousand independent recyclers operates within Beijing. Many are poor migrants from rural villages like Yichang. The recyclers work seven days a week, picking through trash cans and knocking on doors to collect materials from Beijing residents and businesses. The recyclers pedal three-wheeled work bikes stacked high with bales of plastic bottles and cans, bundles of cardboard, and piles of broken electronics and other junk. The recyclers sell their trash at hundreds of recycling businesses crowded around the city landfills.

Beijing's informal recycling sector is efficient. Local waste experts believe that the workers collect about 30 percent of all garbage produced in the city. Despite the relative success of this system, it is not sustainable, or capable of continuing for a long time. As NRDC environmental scientist Judy Li explains,

> The migrants involved in this informal [unregulated] sector earn very little for the effort they spend collecting waste across the city. While urban recycling depends on their hard work, informal collectors are often older, still live in very poor conditions, and have jobs [that] become increasingly difficult as city areas expand.

A woman pedals a tricycle loaded with scavenged Styrofoam packaging through the streets of Beijing. She is heading to the outskirts of the city, where she will sell her load to a recycling business.

BESIEGED BY GARBAGE

Beijing landfills and incinerators are equipped to deal with about 11,000 tons (9,979 metric tons) of garbage a day. However, city residents produce about 18,000 tons (16,329 metric tons) of waste daily. Garbage trucks and private trash haulers take the excess to any of the four hundred or so illegal landfills that form a ring around the city. Few Beijing residents were aware that mountains of trash encircled their city until 2010, when photographer Wang Jiuliang created a documentary called *Beijing Besieged by Waste*.

Those who operate illegal landfills bribe local officials not to punish them or shut down the illegal operations. When Wang threatened to expose this in his documentary, landfill operators threatened him with knives and angry dogs. Once a dozen garbage workers surrounded him and forced him to delete images from his camera.

The illegal dumps attract poor families from across the country. Some live in shanties surrounding the dumps. Others travel to the dumps from other cities and towns. There they pick through the mud, food waste, and animal carcasses, separating metal, plastic, cloth, electronics, and other items not collected by the bike-pedaling recyclers. For the children of the garbage pickers, the dumps are both a workplace and a playground. Barefoot kids, some as young as five years old, dig through trash to help their parents earn a meager living. When not working, children play games among the toxic trash and swim in stagnant pools of water near piles of garbage. Such play is extremely unhealthy, and each year, thousands of children die from diarrhea, pneumonia, viral diseases, and other illnesses contracted at landfills. And the problem is not limited to China. Children work and play in landfills in Indonesia, Ghana, Bangladesh, India, the Philippines, and other poor nations across the globe.

EXPLODING TRASH

Beijing is only one of many mega-cities in China besieged by garbage. Guangzhou, home to more than forty-four million residents, and Shanghai, with twenty-four million residents, face a similar garbage crisis. Even

A 330-foot (100 m) pile of construction debris and other garbage collapsed in Shenzhen, China, in 2015. The avalanche of trash destroyed buildings and killed at least sixty-nine people. Here, rescue workers navigate through the rubble.

smaller cities do too. With a population of around eleven million, Shenzhen is considered a medium-sized city by Chinese standards, but its garbage made international headlines in 2015. On a rainy December afternoon, a 330-foot-high (100 m) mountain of garbage, including dirt, cement chunks, and other construction waste, collapsed and created a massive landslide. Liquefied red mud and debris swallowed thirty-three buildings in a Shenzhen industrial park, including factories, offices, and housing facilities. Geysers of garbage exploded into the air as the debris swept through the city.

By the time the landslide slid to a stop, an area of 450,000 square yards (376,257 sq. m)—equal to seventy football fields—was buried under 33 feet (10 m) of mud and trash. Ninety residents were reported missing, and around four thousand rescue workers joined the days-long effort to save them. While the Chinese government did not release exact figures, at least sixty-nine people died in the disaster.

EXPORTING TOXIC WASTE

Besides producing homegrown trash, China and many even poorer countries import waste from industrialized nations, even though many nations have laws forbidding it. This trash includes toxic materials that wealthy nations don't want to handle. For the world's wealthy countries, it is much less expensive—and safer—to ship waste overseas than to deal with it at home. Poor nations, many of which have high poverty rates, are eager to accept the imported waste because the business generates jobs and much-needed money.

Processing e-waste in particular is big business in poor nations. According to a 2014 report from United Nations University in Tokyo, the e-waste discarded that year contained $52 billion in valuable metals. The gold alone was valued at $11.2 billion. For some nations, it makes economic sense to recover these materials and reuse them. But the EPA estimates that in the United States and other industrialized nations, it is up to ten times cheaper to export e-waste than to recycle it. So every day, thousands of giant shipping containers full of broken and out-of-date electronic devices from the United States, the United Kingdom, Italy, Japan, and other industrialized countries pour into ports in Kenya, Ghana, India, China, and elsewhere.

The sheer amount of electronics destined for the scrap heap is astonishing. In 2014 consumers throughout the world purchased around 277 million desktop computers, 455 million tablets, 250 million televisions, and two billion cell phones. On average, users replace computers and cell phones every two years. Worldwide, e-waste amounts to 54 million tons (49 million metric tons) each year. This waste would fill more than one million heavy trucks in a line 14,300 miles (23,013 km) long.

E-waste contains some of the most hazardous substances on Earth, yet in poor nations, most recyclers work without protective gear. Many use simple tools to separate the valuable materials in e-waste from the plastic cases, wires, and circuit boards. Often working for themselves, with no government health inspection or oversight, recyclers breathe in hazardous fumes and handle toxic substances as they do their jobs.

"A SOUP OF DIOXINS"

The devastating effects of electronics recycling are clearly seen in the West African nation of Ghana. Every day hundreds of shipping containers full of e-waste arrive at the seaport in Ghana's capital city, Accra. Most of the worn-out electronics originates in the United States, Japan, and Europe. Workers wear no protective gear as they use stones, hammers, screwdrivers, and their bare hands to pry apart e-waste. To remove copper from tangled plastic cords, workers burn the cords in open fires, releasing toxic fumes.

Circuit boards and connectors in e-waste are often gold plated. Every cell phone contains about five dollars to ten dollars in gold. The process used to recover the gold is particularly toxic. Workers immerse the components in a highly poisonous brew of cyanide and zinc dust mixed with water. The mixture draws out the gold, and workers use filter paper

E-waste recyclers use their bare hands to extract valuable metals from discarded cell phones at a scrapyard in the Agbogbloshie area of Accra, Ghana. In the process, they breathe toxic fumes and absorb toxins through their skin.

to absorb the precious metal from the solution. This process is inefficient, extracting barely 20 percent of the gold in e-waste.

After the cyanide recovery is complete, workers dump the poisonous liquid directly into local streams, lakes, and rivers. Environmental journalist Tom Zeller Jr. described Ghanaian recycling operations as "toxic ecosystems . . . where acrid [bitter-smelling] plumes of smoke rise from circuit-board smelting [heating and melting] pits, and children bustle amid a soup of dioxins and mercury leaking from mountains of smoldering electronic trash."

Much of the recycling in Ghana takes place at scrapyards in an area of Accra called Agbogbloshie, once an agricultural center. Most of the recyclers there are young males, known in Ghana as e-waste boys. Accra environmentalist Mike Anane described Agbogbloshie in 2015:

> What was once a green and fruitful landscape is now a graveyard
> of plastics and skeletons of abandoned appliances. The e-waste
> boys burn hundreds of kilos of electric cables to extract the copper
> and then resell it for just a few [pennies] per kilogram. The toxic
> fumes rise into the sky, poison the air and then settle on the soil
> and on the vegetables sold at the market.

Most workers in the scrapyards have high levels of lead in their blood, and cancer rates among workers are high. Some of Accra's recyclers die before the age of thirty. However, in a nation where the typical worker earns less than five dollars a day, recycling e-waste can bring in twice the average wage, making this a highly desirable and respectable way to earn a living.

TAKING BACK THE JUNK

Like Ghana, India imports e-waste, but it also produces a lot of e-waste. After China, India is the world's second-largest cell phone market. Indian consumers create more than 500,000 tons (454,000 metric tons) of e-waste each year, and they dump much of it in trash heaps in the country's urban slums. Approximately 1.5 million e-waste pickers sort through that trash.

2. RUBBER
3. SILVER FOIL
4. WIRE
5. PLASTIC

India has passed laws to protect its e-waste recyclers. Here, workers at Attero Recycling in Roorkee, a city in northern India, wear face masks, gloves, and other protective gear as they dismantle old electronics.

While India has one of the world's fastest-growing economies, around 60 percent of the nation's 1.2 billion citizens live on only three dollars a day. Recyclers, who can earn slightly more than the average wage, do not need sophisticated machinery to make money. Like e-waste workers in other poor nations, Indian recyclers are exposed to numerous toxic materials. While most workers understand the hazards, they need to earn a living. As one unnamed worker told the *Huffington Post*, "I know this is really toxic. . . . It might kill me, I know that. But what shall I do about feeding my children?"

The New Delhi–based Chintan Environmental Research and Action Group has an answer to that worker's question. Since 2009 Chintan has organized and trained more than two thousand urban e-waste recyclers. The organization has opened dismantling factories in New Delhi and other Indian cities. Chintan has made the handling of e-waste a "green job" by providing safety training, protective gloves, face masks, and other safety equipment to electronics recyclers.

The Indian government has also begun to deal with e-waste cleanup. In 2011 it passed a law requiring large, global electronics manufacturers to run "take-back" programs in Indian cities. The programs include e-waste collection centers where people can turn in their used electronics. The government also regulates recycling businesses to make sure that workers dismantling e-waste have safety equipment.

THE BASEL CONVENTION

Exporting e-waste is actually illegal under international law according to a 1989 UN treaty called the Basel Convention. After the treaty was enacted, the European Union (EU, a political and economic alliance of European nations) adopted rules that bring EU nations into compliance with the Basel Convention. The regulations require electronics manufacturers to collect e-waste and recycle it within Europe safely and responsibly. But the rules have loopholes. For instance, if the e-waste can be reused or refurbished, it can be legally exported. Many European businesses falsely label their e-waste as reusable materials to take advantage of this loophole. And some groups steal e-waste from European collection points and sell it to recyclers in poor nations, mostly in Africa and Asia. In the end, only one-third of Europe's e-waste is properly recycled.

The United States—the world's largest producer of e-waste—is the only industrialized nation that has not signed onto the Basel Convention. Since complying with the convention would cut into business profits, powerful and well-funded groups such as the US Chamber of Commerce (a business trade association), big electronics manufacturers, and the trade group Institute of Scrap Recycling Industries have lobbied against signing on. They have so far been successful in ensuring that the United States doesn't agree to the convention.

TRACKING E-WASTE

No federal US agency oversees e-waste recycling, but many states operate e-waste programs in tandem with private recyclers. As a result, millions of

PASSING THE RADIOACTIVE BUCK

When nuclear technology first emerged in the mid-twentieth century, many facilities that produced nuclear weapons and nuclear power simply dumped radioactive waste into open-air pits and canyons. Other groups dumped waste into waterways. After the dangers of nuclear waste became known, nations searched for places to bury the waste deep underground. But when nuclear regulatory agencies identify possible sites for waste disposal, communities often fight back. For instance, the governor of Nevada vetoed a plan to bury waste inside the state's Yucca Mountain in 2002, although the US Congress overrode the veto. (The project has yet to begin, and Nevada residents are still trying to block it.)

The United States has considered shipping its nuclear waste overseas. One 2011 plan involved sending US and Japanese waste to the remote desert in the Asian nation of Mongolia, but Mongolian citizens protested and the plan fell apart. On various occasions since the mid-twentieth century, industrialized nations have illegally dumped nuclear waste in poor nations, such as Nigeria in Africa. But since shipping radioactive waste can be more dangerous than simply letting it sit in storage, it usually remains where it's produced.

US consumers voluntarily recycle their e-waste; around 40 percent of the 3.1 million tons (2.8 million metric tons) of e-waste generated annually in the United States is recycled. Look online to see if your community has an e-waste drop-off site.

The Basel Action Network (BAN), a nonprofit organization based in Seattle, Washington, and devoted to ending the trade in toxic waste, is working to better track e-waste recycling. In 2014 BAN launched the e-Trash Transparency Project to discover where e-waste goes after it reaches US recyclers. BAN placed two hundred small GPS tracking devices into old computer printers and monitors and delivered them to various e-waste recyclers around the country. The GPS devices allowed BAN to follow the equipment wherever it went.

In a two-year study, the group found that about one-third of all tracked e-waste—about 376,800 tons (341,827 metric tons) annually—ended up overseas, while two-thirds was recycled in the United States. BAN found that sixty-five US recyclers were shipping e-waste to China, Thailand, Pakistan, Taiwan, Mexico, and Kenya. These shipments are illegal on several levels. First, most of the nations receiving the waste have laws that ban the import of e-waste from industrialized nations. And once shipping containers carrying e-waste enter international waters, the US recyclers responsible for the shipments are in violation of the Basel Ban, even though the United States has not formally signed the treaty.

The export of e-waste deprives US recyclers of a large share of the e-waste market. US businesses must pay workers a minimum wage and follow federal guidelines for worker safety. Because of these requirements, they can't recycle e-waste as cheaply as recyclers in poor nations, which generally have few environmental or worker safety laws. BAN executive director Jim Puckett comments, "Toxic e-waste is flowing off our shores every day to substandard operations [overseas], harming people and the environment across the globe. Meanwhile, these exports deprive our own nation of green jobs and make it difficult for responsible [US] electronics recyclers to compete and survive."

BUILDING SOLUTIONS

Global e-waste is on the rise, with an expected growth rate of 33 percent between 2014 and 2018. To counter this trend, environmentalists encourage consumers to replace their electronics far less often and to recycle them at local drop-off sites. Many cities, stores, and manufacturers accept devices for recycling. Check online for more information about recycling in your area. By realizing the environmental impact of every cell phone, video game console, and computer, consumers can work together to reduce the amount of e-waste they create.

CHAPTER 6
OCEANS OF PLASTIC

Imagine an ocean full of garbage as far as the eye can see. That's what Charles J. Moore, an heir to the Hancock Oil Company family fortune, discovered after taking part in a yacht race from Los Angeles to Hawaii in 1997. When the race ended, Moore decided to sail back home to California through the North Pacific Gyre. The gyre is a massive area of clockwise ocean currents, slowly spinning around the North Pacific Ocean.

Sailors usually avoid the gyre because it has very little wind. This is due to a climate feature called the North Pacific subtropical high-pressure zone. The combination of sluggish currents and air under high pressure produces what sailors call doldrums, regions of dead calm. In previous centuries, doldrums sometimes stranded sailing ships in the ocean for weeks.

Moore had a motor on his yacht to help him traverse the dead calm. He was a surfer, scuba diver, and ship's captain. He had seen the ocean at its most glorious and most threatening and did not expect much excitement from his journey through the isolated North Pacific Gyre. But Moore was shocked when he passed through the open sea in the center of the gyre. According to Moore, every time he stepped out onto the deck, "there were shampoo caps and soap bottles and plastic bags and fishing floats as far as I could see. Here I was in the middle of the ocean, and there was nowhere I could go to avoid the plastic."

In one 10-mile (16 km) section of the gyre, the surface of the water was dominated by an estimated six million floating plastic bags. Moore and his crew saw bags with logos from major corporations, including Sears, Bristol Farms, Taco Bell, and El Pollo Loco. Some of the logos on the bags were more than ten years old, yet the plastic had barely deteriorated. When Moore returned home, he founded Algalita Marine Research and Education in Long Beach, California, to publicize the problem of plastics in the ocean. Since he had little scientific experience, he hired chemists, biologists, and other scientists to conduct research into the problem.

One of the first steps was to figure out the amount of plastic in the gyre. So in 1999, Moore purchased a research ship and returned to the garbage-strewn gyre with an all-volunteer crew. Researchers skimmed the surface of the water with fine-mesh collecting nets. Traveling across 7,500 miles (12,070 km) of ocean, the crew counted approximately one million pieces of plastic per square mile (2.5 sq. km). Since then, Algalita has worked tirelessly to protect the marine environment and to educate the public on the impact of plastic pollution in the ocean.

A FLOATING LANDFILL

The North Pacific Gyre has been called a trash vortex, a floating landfill, and the Great Pacific Garbage Patch. It is actually several distinct patches covering about 270,000 square miles (700,000 sq. km), an area about the size of Texas.

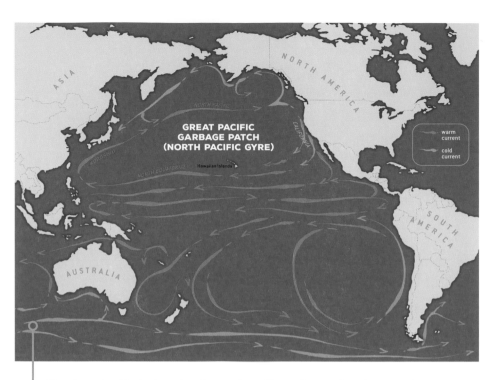

The Great Pacific Garbage Patch contains millions of tons of trash, most of it plastic.

The North Pacific Gyre is one of five gyres in Earth's oceans. Others are the South Pacific Gyre, the North Atlantic Gyre, the South Atlantic Gyre, and the Indian Ocean Gyre. The weak winds and slowly spinning currents in gyres have long collected old pieces of shipwrecks called flotsam. Since the 1950s, the gyres have also been pulling in tons of trash, mostly plastic.

Around 90 percent of all trash in the ocean is plastic. In February 2015, the journal *Science* released a study that showed that an average of 8.8 million tons (8 million metric tons) of plastic enters the ocean annually. Jenna Jambeck, one of the study's authors, put that number in perspective: "It's five [grocery] bags filled with plastic for every foot of coastline in the world."

About 80 percent of plastic in the ocean originates on land. Wind and rain carry plastic trash into waterways and into the ocean from littered streets, storm drains, landfills, illegal dumps, and beaches. Other plastic debris comes from cruise ships, fishing boats, oil rigs, and other vessels. This garbage includes nets and other fishing gear, plastic ropes, and buoys, either purposely or accidentally dropped overboard. Sometimes, containers full of consumer goods fall off ships during storms and hurricanes, littering the ocean with plastic products. In 1992 a container filled with thousands of plastic rubber ducks was lost at sea in a powerful storm. Some of the plastic toys are still being found in the North Pacific Gyre. Another storm, in 1990, sent eighty thousand Nike sneakers and work boots into the Pacific Ocean.

Whatever the source of the plastic, currents eventually deposit much of it into one of the five major ocean gyres. The Great Pacific Garbage Patch contains 3.5 million tons (3.1 million metric tons) of plastic trash extending 9 feet (2.7 m) below the ocean's surface. Researchers have concluded that in some parts of the North Pacific Gyre, for every 2.2 pounds (1 kg) of plankton (tiny sea creatures) and other organic matter, the seawater contains more than 13 pounds (6 kg) of plastic.

BILLIONS OF NURDLES

A major percentage of the debris in the North Pacific Gyre consists of tiny plastic pellets called nurdles. These are smaller than pencil erasers, about 0.2 inches (5 millimeters) in diameter. Passing boaters can't even see them. Manufacturers use nurdles to make thousands of different kinds of plastic items, including buckets, food storage containers, and grocery bags. It takes six hundred melted nurdles to make one plastic bottle.

Worldwide, manufacturers produce around 250 billion pounds (113 billion kg) of nurdles annually. Ships, trains, trucks, and airplanes then carry them to plastics factories. They are so lightweight that they often blow around like dust, and they are difficult to control. In fact, they make their way into the environment during almost every part of transportation, manufacturing, and shipping, even with good controls in place. When Moore visited a plastic pipe factory in 2004, he walked through an area where railcars were unloading nurdles. He noticed that his pants cuffs were filled with the fine plastic pellets. He later saw windblown nurdles piled up like a snowdrift against a fence. Nurdles sometimes fall into the water at seaports, when containers filled with nurdles are loaded and unloaded.

Others enter the ocean during accidents at sea. In 2012 six shipping containers of nurdles fell off a Hong Kong freighter. In that incident, 168 tons (152 metric tons) of the plastic pellets went into the ocean.

While their name makes nurdles sound harmless, the pellets are extremely dangerous to ocean life. The ocean food chain begins with plankton, a crucial source of food for larger sea creatures, such as fish, squid, and twelve species of whales. Without plankton, these creatures would starve. Some species of plankton attempt to eat nurdles because they resemble fish eggs and other food. Nurdles choke the plankton to death, leaving animals that feed on plankton with reduced food supplies. And when fish eat nurdles, they develop digestive problems and either starve or suffer from extreme constipation. Moore points out that tiny nurdles have a huge impact. He says, "It's not the big trash on the beach [that is such a big problem]. It's the fact that the whole [environment] is becoming mixed with these plastic particles. What are they doing to us? We're breathing them, the fish are eating them, they're in our hair, they're in our skin."

MICROPLASTICS IN THE FOOD CHAIN

Nurdles are only one type of plastic choking sea life. When large plastic items—soda bottles, lawn chairs, car parts, and other junk—float in the ocean, the objects eventually break down. This happens when sunlight interacts with the plastic in a process called photodegradation. Taking anywhere from a few months to five hundred years, photodegradation turns large plastic objects into tiny particles. In the ocean, these plastic bits, called microplastics, turn seawater into a murky soup.

The basic elements of plastics are called polymers. Polymers last forever. The microorganisms that normally break down organic matter do not feed on them. As science reporter Thomas Morton explains, "except for the slim handful of plastics designed specifically to biodegrade, every synthetic molecule ever made still exists. And except for the small percentage that gets caught in a net or washes up on a shore, every chunk of plastic that's dropped into the Pacific makes its way to the center of a Gyre and is floating there right now."

USING ART TO INFORM

Most people are not aware of the Great Pacific Garbage Patch because it is out of sight. But a number of artists are using their creative talents to shine a light on the harm that plastic is causing in the marine environment.

In Bandon, Oregon, for example, a colorful sculpture known as *Henry the Fish (below)* looks, from afar, like a typical piece of art. However, upon closer examination, viewers can see that *Henry the Fish* consists of garbage picked up on the local beach. The sculpture's bright orange-and-yellow scales are made from cigarette lighters, beach shovels, toothbrushes, and other plastic trash. Henry's large lips are pieces of Styrofoam and abandoned buoys. His shiny eyes are made from water bottles from the 2008 Beijing Olympics, which eventually washed from Chinese landfills to the shore in Oregon—all the way across the Pacific Ocean.

Henry the Fish was the idea of Angela Haseltine Pozzi, executive director and lead artist at the Bandon environmental group Washed Ashore. Other Washed Ashore sculptures made from plastic trash include *Lidia the Seal*, made from netting, ropes, and buoys, and the *Musical Sea Star*, constructed from glass bottles. Washed Ashore marketing director Frank Rocco explains the importance of the project: "[Its] purpose is to remind the public that much of today's plastic products should be recycled, re-purposed and re-used so that it will be less of a threat to sea life that lives on the ocean and also to wildlife that lives out of water."

Polymers work their way up the food chain from small creatures to larger animals. For instance, jellyfish eat microplastics, taking polymers into their bodies. Small fish eat the jellyfish, and larger fish eat the small fish. The polymers continue to travel up the food chain to the biggest, fattiest fish, such as swordfish and tuna. And individual polymer molecules act as sponges for toxic chemicals from other sources. They absorb PCBs, TCP, and dioxin from oil, pesticides, insecticides, and other industrial fluids in waterways.

Swordfish and tuna contain high levels of PCBs and dioxin, chemicals directly traced to microplastics and nurdles. This is particularly troubling since canned tuna is the second most popular food fish in the United States. And because the toxins in the fish are endocrine disrupters, they can cause fatal tumors and liver problems in humans who eat the fish.

MORE PLASTIC THAN FISH

Plastic in the ocean is not confined to gyres. Beaches, islands, and areas close to shore all contain plastic trash. Seabirds often mistake brightly colored bits of plastic for food or eat plastic items by accident. Some birds eat plastic bags, thinking they are squid or fish. Young chicks in the nest become bloated with plastic when their parents unintentionally feed them debris.

In 2015 a group of Australian researchers analyzed scientific data on 186 species of seabirds. The researchers determined that 90 percent of all seabirds have ingested some form of plastic. One of the researchers, Denise Hardesty, once found two hundred pieces of plastic inside the digestive system of one bird. She noted some of the items she has found: "everything from cigarette lighters . . . to bottle caps to model cars. I've found toys."

Marine plastic kills an estimated one million seabirds every year. The debris also kills hundreds of thousands of sea turtles and marine mammals, including dolphins and whales. Like birds, these creatures often mistake plastic for food. In 2011 a young sperm whale was found floating dead near Greece. The animal's belly was so distended that scientists at

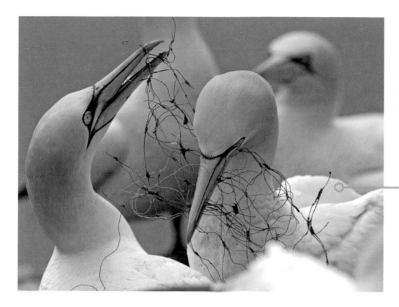

These northern gannets in Helgoland, Germany, are tangled in a plastic fishing net. Every year, about one million seabirds die from ingesting plastic such as this.

first thought it had eaten a giant squid. A report by the *Journal of the American Cetacean [Whale] Society* describes what researchers found during a necropsy (animal autopsy):

> All our "civilization" was in the stomach of this whale. [Dozens] of big compacted plastic bags used for garbage or construction materials, all kinds of plastic for anything we can buy in a supermarket, plastic ropes, pieces of nets, even a plastic bag with full address and telephone number of a [fast-food] restaurant in the town of Thessaloniki (located some 500 km [310 miles] further north).

Whales and plastic attracted more media attention in 2016 when thirteen male sperm whales beached themselves and died near the town of Tönning, Germany, on the shores of the North Sea. When scientists conducted necropsies on the beached sperm whales, they found their stomachs filled with plastic debris. The items included dozens of plastic bags, a piece of a plastic bucket, a 42-foot (13 m) piece of shrimp fishing net, and a 2-foot (61 cm) segment of plastic from a car engine cover.

Researchers are unsure why the whales beached themselves and do not believe the ingested garbage killed them. However, plastic can hurt whales in numerous ways. It can disrupt a whale's digestion. The plastic provides a feeling of fullness and diminishes the animal's appetite, reducing its rate of growth. In the worst cases, plastic completely blocks the digestive tract or sharp pieces of debris cause internal injuries, such as a rupture of the stomach. Then the whale starves and suffers in extreme pain.

Scientists expect the problem to get worse. By the middle of the twenty-first century, the world will produce three times more plastic than it did in 2015. Researchers at the World Economic Forum have arrived at a startling conclusion: By 2025 the oceans are expected to contain 1.1 tons (1 metric ton) of plastic for every 3.3 tons (3 metric tons) of fish. By 2050 the ocean will hold more plastic than fish.

DISMANTLING THE GARBAGE PATCH

Researchers say that once plastic is in the ocean, it is nearly impossible to remove. Inventor Boyan Slat, from Delft, Netherlands, is challenging that belief with a system called the Ocean Cleanup Array. The idea for the invention came to Slat in 2011, when he was sixteen years old. Slat was scuba diving off the coast of Greece, where he saw more plastic bags than fish in the sea. He was distressed when people told him that the problem had no solution.

Slat explained why cleanup is considered impossible, using the North Pacific Gyre as an example: "Most people have this image of an island of trash that you can almost walk on, but that's not what it's like. It stretches for millions of square kilometers—if you went there to try and clean [it] up by ship it would take thousands of years." Faced with this problem, Slat, who excels at solving puzzles, came up with an idea: rather than chasing trash, he wanted to harness the natural currents of the ocean to deliver the trash to giant collectors.

The Ocean Cleanup Array, which is still in the design phase, consists of a floating barrier 62 miles (100 km) long and a few feet thick. It looks

Boyan Slat was a teen when he developed the Ocean Cleanup Array, a structure designed to extract plastic from the ocean. Here, Slat stands before a prototype (model) of his invention off the coast of Holland in 2016.

like the booms used to skim oil off the water after an oil spill. In Slat's plan, the barrier will ride along the ocean surface catching plastic carried on the current. Sea life will pass under the barrier. The device will funnel the trash to a central platform for extraction. Ships will carry the collected plastic to shore for recycling. Although the design does not remove microplastics from the water, Slat says that removing large pieces of plastic is a good start toward cleaning up seawater. With less of the big plastic to break down in the water, the ocean will theoretically gain fewer microplastics over time.

Slat entered his project in a science fair at Delft University of Technology, where it won the prize for Best Technical Design in 2012. This honor inspired him to found an organization called the Ocean Cleanup and to put his project to the test. Slat gave a TEDx Talk, a showcase for new ideas, and the speech went viral on YouTube. The talk also caught the attention of American tech entrepreneur Marc Benioff, who funded a 2015 mission to test the Ocean Cleanup Array in the Great Pacific Garbage Patch. During the mission, the crew measured the extent of the trash and mapped the dirtiest locations with GPS and a smartphone app. Slat is planning to build a 1-mile (1.6 km) prototype of the Ocean Cleanup Array and put it to work near Japan in 2017.

MR. TRASH WHEEL EATS PLASTIC

The environmental group Waterfront Partnership of Baltimore found a unique way to address the problem of trash flowing into the city's Inner Harbor from storm sewers. In 2014 the group set up a waterwheel in the mouth of the Jones Falls River—a watershed that drains 58 square miles (150 sq. km) of land outside Baltimore. Called the Inner Harbor Water Wheel—and known as Mr. Trash Wheel to locals—the device catches trash as it enters the harbor. The Waterfront Partnership describes how Mr. Trash Wheel works: "The river's current provides power to turn the water wheel, which lifts trash and debris from the water and deposits it into a dumpster barge. When there isn't enough water current, a solar panel array provides additional power to keep the machine running."

During its first two years of operation, Mr. Trash Wheel removed more than 257,000 plastic bottles, 327,000 polystyrene food containers, 173,000 grocery bags, 244,000 chip bags, and 7.4 million cigarette butts from the harbor. Mr. Trash Wheel even has its own Twitter account and live feed on the Internet.

More than seventy scientists who looked at the design concluded that it was a practical way to remove plastic from the ocean, and Slat is incredibly optimistic. He says, "With a single system, in 10 years time, approximately half the Great Pacific Garbage Patch can be cleaned up."

TOP PLASTIC POLLUTERS

Slat understands that the best way to halt plastic pollution in the ocean is to stop it at its source. To do so, scientists need to find out where all the plastic is coming from. Jenna Jambeck and a team of researchers tried to provide an answer by analyzing data on population density, solid waste production, and other statistics from the world's 192 coastal countries. The research, compiled in a 2015 study, contained some surprises. It revealed that while the United States produces the most plastic, it ranks twentieth on the list of the most plastic-polluting nations. However, the United States is the only industrialized country on the list. Other industrialized nations are doing a better job at reducing plastic pollution.

The top plastic polluter in the world is China, which dumped 5 billion pounds (2.2 billion kg) of plastic waste into the ocean in 2010, followed by

Indonesia, which dumped around 2 billion pounds (0.9 billion kg). Other top countries include the Philippines, Vietnam, Thailand, and Egypt. In all, the top twenty countries on the list accounted for 83 percent of all mismanaged plastic waste. These statistics are bad news, because most of the top producers of plastic pollution are poor countries, without the financial resources to effectively manage waste and with few or poorly enforced environmental laws.

SEVEN HUNDRED PIECES OF PLASTIC

Anyone looking around their home, school, or place of business will see hundreds of plastic objects. Almost every single thing within view—from wastebaskets to chairs, from television sets to computers—is also found floating in the ocean. A 2014 study revealed about 5.2 trillion pieces of plastic floating in the world's oceans. That's about 700 pieces for every human on the planet.

To stop the flow of trash, an increasing number of communities around the world are discouraging the use of plastic bags, either by charging a tax for using the bags or by banning them outright. However, the plastic industry works tirelessly to defeat such taxes and bans because they cut into sales and cut down on profits.

As with other trash tragedies, it is up to individuals to change their behavior. Shoppers can reduce plastic pollution by taking reusable cloth bags to the store. They can buy fewer prepackaged foods and beverages and instead prepare more food from scratch at home. They can make sure that all plastic trash is properly disposed of or put into recycling bins. And they can work with friends, family, and coworkers to volunteer to clean up plastic trash in local parks, along highways, and on beaches so that it doesn't end up in nearby waters.

Life on Earth depends on healthy oceans. Fish, birds, and sea mammals must be protected from the garbage that is destroying their marine habitat. Humans caused the plastic problem, and humans can solve it.

CHAPTER 7
SPACE JUNK

Humans have covered Planet Earth with trash and toxic waste. But did you know that we're polluting outer space too? It all started in the 1950s, when the United States and the Soviet Union (1922–1991, a union of fifteen countries that included Russia) began sending satellites into space. In 1957 the Soviet Union launched its first two satellites, and the United States launched its first satellite in 1958.

On March 17, 1958, the United States launched its second satellite, a small research satellite called Vanguard 1. The satellite was a 3.2-pound (1.5 kg) aluminum sphere, 6.4 inches (16 cm) in diameter. Six 12-inch (30 cm) antennae projected from the surface of the satellite. Vanguard 1 was historic for several reasons: circling above Earth at 2,440 miles (3,926 km),

A NASA illustration shows a research satellite orbiting Earth. The space around our planet is filled with about one thousand operational satellites and about twenty-six hundred zombie (nonoperational) satellites. If and when these vehicles crash into one another, they break apart into thousands of pieces of space junk.

Vanguard 1 achieved the then-highest altitude of any space vehicle. It was also the first solar-powered satellite.

Vanguard 1 collected information about Earth's shape and gravitational field. The satellite's mission ended in 1965, when its solar-powered communications system failed. But in the twenty first century, Vanguard 1 is still in space, circling Earth once every 133 minutes. In 2008, on the satellite's fiftieth anniversary, the US National Aeronautics and Space Administration (NASA) noted that the spacecraft had completed more than 197,000 Earth orbits, traveling more than 6 billion miles (10 billion km). Scientists calculate that the grapefruit-size Vanguard 1 will continue to travel around Earth for another 240 years before finally falling from its orbit and reentering Earth's atmosphere.

ZOMBIES AND OTHER JUNK

Vanguard 1 is the oldest zombie (nonoperational) satellite traveling around Earth, but it is certainly not alone. About twenty-six hundred zombie satellites are orbiting Earth. And zombies make up just a tiny percentage of all the human-made junk in space. Other junk includes nuts and bolts dropped by astronauts on space walks; fragments of metal, glass, plastic, and paint broken off from old satellites; and sections of rockets used to launch space vehicles.

In 2016 scientists with NASA were tracking more than twenty-three thousand pieces of orbital debris larger than 4 inches (10 cm) across. Hundreds of thousands of pieces of debris are too small to track. Whatever the size of the orbital debris, it travels fast up to 4 miles (6.4 km) per second, or 17,500 miles (28,163 km) per hour. At this speed, even the tiniest chip of paint can cause severe damage to working satellites. When a 0.4-inch (1 cm) object traveling through space hits something, the damage is equivalent to a 550-pound (249 kg) rock hitting a car traveling at 60 miles (97 km) per hour. Such an impact can destroy crucial

AVALANCHE IN SPACE

In 1978 NASA scientist Donald Kessler described a theoretical situation in which two objects collide in space and break apart. The resulting debris collides with other objects, shattering them into fragments, resulting in even more debris. More collisions follow, with the creation of more and more debris—all of which threatens operational spacecraft. The scenario, known as the Kessler syndrome, could wipe out satellites needed for critical jobs on Earth.

In 2016 Ben Greene, chief executive of the Australian Space Environment Research Centre, determined that the Kessler syndrome is a very real concern: "The most pessimistic mathematical model says that we are within five years of having a 50-50 chance that a catastrophic avalanche of collisions will occur any day. The most optimistic model says we've got 25 years."

Some scientists say that the Kessler syndrome is already happening, but in slow motion. Each small collision results in an uptick in the amount of space junk and the number of other small collisions. While not as dramatic as Greene's "catastrophic avalanche," the end result will ultimately be the same.

components on space vehicles. And each crash creates hundreds of new pieces of threatening debris. For example, the accidental 2009 collision of US communications satellite Iridium 33 and the Russian zombie satellite Kosmos 2251 created thousands of pieces of space debris larger than 4 inches in diameter.

Most orbital debris is the unintentional by-product of space exploration. However, in 2007 China sent shock waves through the space industry when its military deliberately destroyed a Chinese weather satellite with an antisatellite (ASAT) weapon launched by a ballistic missile. ASATs are designed to destroy enemy defense and spy satellites, and China wanted to test its ASAT capabilities. The ASAT blew the weather satellite to pieces, creating around 950 pieces of space junk. Nicholas Johnson, NASA's chief scientist for orbital debris, commented on the test: "Any of these debris has the potential for seriously disrupting or terminating the mission of operational spacecraft in low Earth orbit. This satellite breakup represents the most prolific and serious fragmentation in the course of 50 years of space operations."

MOVING TARGET

Johnson noted that the debris from the Chinese test threatened the International Space Station (ISS), the largest artificial structure in orbit. Aerospace companies built sections of the station on Earth, and space shuttles carried them into orbit. Astronauts assembled the sections in space. The first section of the ISS went into space in 1998.

At a cost of $150 billion to build and maintain through 2015, the ISS is one of the most complex and expensive items ever made by human hands. Astronauts use the station as a research laboratory. At any given time, the crew consists of three to six astronauts and scientists from several nations, including the United States, Russia, France, Germany, Japan, and the United Kingdom.

Space junk has hit the ISS numerous times, but the damage has so far been minor. For instance, in May 2016, a flake of orbiting paint smashed into one of the craft's 2-inch-thick (5 cm) windows. In a photo tweeted by British astronaut Tim Peake, a tiny crack on the surface of the window glass is obvious.

The ISS is the most heavily shielded spacecraft ever flown. Bumpers made of layers of metal and bulletproof fabric protect important ISS components, such as its living compartments and high-pressure oxygen tanks. The multilayer shields are designed to deflect or absorb the impact of small particles of space junk.

The bumpers offer little protection against larger objects, however. A piece of debris the size of a baseball could blast the ISS into pieces. Controllers on the ground monitor space junk, and if they see debris headed toward the ISS, the crew maneuvers the station out of its way. If the chance of collision is strong, the crew retreats to a Soyuz space capsule docked at the ISS. The Russian built Soyuz can carry the crew back to Earth in about three and a half hours in an emergency.

TRACKING ORBITAL DEBRIS

An estimated twelve hundred active commercial satellites are orbiting Earth. Some of them relay telephone or television signals. Others aid in weather forecasting, national defense, navigation, and scientific research. Satellites cost anywhere from $20 million to $3 billion each, and all active satellites together are worth around $1 trillion. Because satellites are so important, government agencies spend a great deal of time and money tracking space debris. When trackers see that a piece of debris is headed toward an active satellite, they notify satellite controllers on the ground, who remotely maneuver the satellite to avoid a collision.

In the United States, the task of tracking space junk falls to the Space Surveillance Network (SSN), operated by the US Department of Defense. Using radar, telescopes, and high-powered cameras, the SSN can track objects as small as 2 inches (5 cm) across. The SSN often consults with space-tracking agencies from other nations, such as Australia's Space Environment Research Centre, a world leader in tracking space debris.

CLEANING UP SPACE JUNK

Some scientists say that to remove the threat to satellites and other space vehicles, we must devise methods for removing space junk from orbit. NASA researchers have proposed arming the ISS or satellites with lasers that could shoot down large pieces of junk. The lasers would fire ten thousand pulses per second, partially melt pieces of space debris, and push them into Earth's atmosphere. There, as the debris fell toward Earth, it would grow extremely hot as it rubbed against the air. It would disintegrate and burn up before hitting the ground. A laser debris-removal system has yet to be built, but if it were, it could potentially destroy one piece of debris every five minutes, cleaning up one hundred thousand pieces of space junk each year. In little more than four years of deployment, the system could remove the most troubling debris circling Earth.

The European Space Agency (ESA) has another idea for removing clutter from orbit. The agency's first debris removal mission is scheduled for 2021. On this mission, a spacecraft nicknamed the garbage truck will rendezvous with and capture a zombie satellite. The garbage truck will use robotic arms or a large net to grab the satellite. The garbage truck will then push the satellite into Earth's atmosphere, where it will burn up. Robin Biesbroek of the ESA explains the difficulties involved:

> We have to take many things into account . . . such as how costly
> [the garbage truck] will be to develop, how [adaptable] it will be
> to changing circumstances, how heavy it is, how strongly it can
> hold the debris, how easy it is to perform a second try if the first
> try fails, and how much it fulfills the requirement to not create
> any extra debris. . . . Many technologies of this mission are new,
> as nobody has ever removed debris from orbit.

Researchers at Texas A&M University in College Station are designing a system called the Space Sweeper with Sling-Sat (4S). This cleanup craft

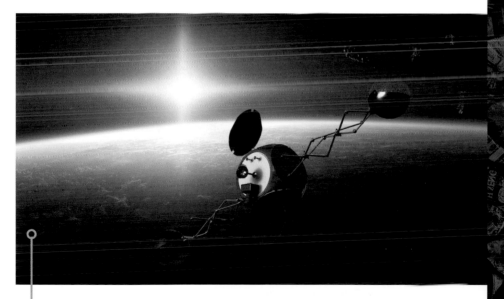

Engineers at space agencies and universities are designing remotely controlled vehicles that might be able to clean up space junk. This one, the Space Sweeper with Sling-Sat, would fling debris back into Earth's atmosphere, where it would naturally burn up and disintegrate. The flinging motion would also propel the Sweeper through space.

would travel from one piece of space junk to the next, deorbiting debris one object at a time. The 4S designers note that a cleanup system like the ESA garbage truck would require massive amounts of fuel to travel between pieces of space junk. The 4S would solve this problem by capturing a piece of debris and flinging it down into the atmosphere. The momentum from the flinging motion would propel the 4S to the next piece of space junk, minimizing fuel use. Researcher Jonathan Missel explains the urgency behind his work:

> It is well understood that we are past the point of no return. Relying solely on improved tracking and avoidance [of space junk] is not enough. . . . It is simply a technical form of sticking your head in the sand and crossing your fingers. We are at a point where the problem needs to be solved, with active removal, not just avoided.

While Missel's statement is accurate, no government or space agency is yet committed to a full-scale cleanup of space junk. Such an undertaking would be enormously expensive.

WHAT GOES UP

Can space junk land on Earth? In January 2016, three air tanks from a Russian satellite fell from space and landed in a town in the Southeast Asian nation of Vietnam. Unlike most pieces of space junk, the tanks hadn't burned up as they fell through Earth's atmosphere. The junk didn't hit anyone or damage any structures on the ground. But local residents reported that before the objects struck, they heard a sound like thunder.

The largest piece of space junk ever to plunge toward Earth, without making landfall, was Mir, a defunct Russian space station. In March 2001, the 286,600-pound (130,000 kg) craft provided a light show to those on the ground when it burned up high in the atmosphere and broke apart into

In January 2001, a section of a rocket used to launch a US spacecraft fell back to Earth instead of burning up high in the atmosphere. It landed in the desert of Saudi Arabia.

fifteen hundred large fragments. The blazing bits, traveling faster than the speed of sound, created loud explosions called sonic booms.

WHAT TO DO NOW?

Photos of Earth taken from outer space are among the most important gifts that NASA has made to humanity. One of the most famous photos, called *Blue Marble*, is a 2012 picture of Earth taken from a satellite. The deep blue waters of the ocean, encircled by swirling white clouds, make Earth resemble a toy marble. The blue-green planet hangs in the dry, black emptiness of space.

Blue Marble makes one thing abundantly clear: we have only one Earth. No more Blue Marbles are within humanity's reach, and if we continue to trash this one, we will no longer have a safe, nourishing, and healthy place to live. Whether the trash we are dealing with is space junk,

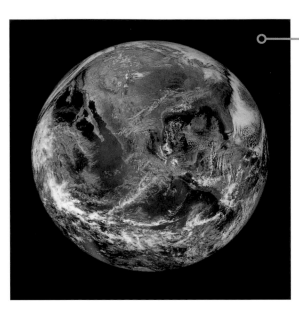

The photograph *Blue Marble*, taken by a satellite in 2012, shows the marvelous beauty of Earth's oceans, lands, and cloud-filled skies. Earth is the only planet in our solar system known to support life. If we continue to trash our planet, it may no longer be able to sustain life.

leaky landfills, plastic in the ocean, or toxic and nuclear waste, cleaning up Earth is one of the most important tasks we face.

YOUTH LEAD THE WAY

While the situation might seem hopeless, young people across the globe are seeking solutions to the problems of mountains of trash and hazardous waste. The first step in finding answers to these troublesome problems is to become informed and to explain the issues to others, especially parents and family. After all, the habits of individual consumers cause most trash problems. If millions of people convinced their family members to buy less stuff and to properly recycle what they did buy, they could make a huge dent in the trash problem. Bringing cloth grocery bags to the store and reusable containers to restaurants for leftovers can also make a difference, as can avoiding processed food wrapped in plastic packaging. If more people cooked meals from fruits and vegetables grown in home gardens, we could keep landfills from overflowing with plastic containers while slowing climate change.

Concerned citizens can raise their voices through organizations working to stop the trashing of Planet Earth. The Ocean Conservancy

Teen volunteers clean up trash in a Detroit, Michigan, neighborhood. Each individual can make a difference in tackling the global garbage glut.

(www.oceanconservancy.org) and the Plastic Pollution Coalition (www.plasticpollutioncoalition.org) are fighting for trash-free seas. The two million members of the National Resources Defense Council (www.nrdc.org) work to reduce the use of toxic chemicals, slow climate change, and clean up Earth's air and water. The World Wildlife Fund (www.worldwildlife.org) tries to save endangered species. That work involves fighting the illegal dumping of toxic trash, which can kill plants and animals.

The Internet offers an abundance of answers to the debris debacle. And seeking solutions together is so much more constructive than brooding hopelessly alone. The garbage isn't going to pick up itself, and anyone who eats, drinks, and purchases consumer goods owes it to the planet to become part of the solution rather than remaining part of the problem.

SOURCES NOTES

5   Katie Allen, "Torrential Rainstorm Sends Plastic Pollution into the Ocean," Story of Stuff Project, accessed July 19, 2016, http://storyofstuff.org/blog/torrential-rainstorm-sends-plastic-pollution-into-the-ocean.

17 Kaley Beins and Stephen Lester, *Superfund: Polluters Pay So Children Can Play*, Center for Health, Environment & Justice, December 2015, http://chej.org/wp-content/uploads/Superfund-35th-Anniversary-Report1.pdf.

20–21 Edward Humes, *Garbology: Our Dirty Love Affair with Trash* (New York: Avery, 2012), 14.

21 Ibid., 18.

24 Richard Weizel, "A School on a Dump Site Divides Hamden," *New York Times*, June 30, 2002, http://www.nytimes.com/2002/06/30/nyregion/a-school-on-a-dump-site-divides-hamden.html?pagewanted=all.

25 G. Fred Lee and Anne Jones-Lee, *Assessment of the Performance of Engineered Waste Containment Barriers* (Washington, DC: National Academies, 2009), 2.

29 Carlos Granada, "Sun Valley High-Tech Plant Looks to Separate Treasures from Trash," *ABC7*, April 8, 2016, http://abc7.com/news/sun-valley-high-tech-plant-looks-to-separate-treasures-from-trash/1283462.

32 Noelle Nicholas, "Silverton, Colorado: State of Emergency Declared following Massive Toxic Spill," *Inquisitr*, August 11, 2015, http://www.inquisitr.com/2326137/silverton-colorado-toxic-spill/.

32 Julie Turkewitz, "Environmental Agency Uncorks Its Own Toxic Water Spill at Colorado Mines," *New York Times*, August 10, 2015, http://www.nytimes.com/2015/08/11/us/durango-colorado-mine-spill-environmental-protection-agency.html?smid=tw-nytimes&_r=0.

33   John Hickenlooper, quoted in Nicholas, "Silverton, Colorado."

33 Tom Myers, quoted in Brennan Linsley, Lindsay Whitehurst, Colleen Slevin, Ivan Moreno, Susan Montoya Bryan, and Brian Skoloff, "EPA Spill of Toxic Waste Could Be Long-Term Calamity," *Huffington Post*, August 12, 2015, http://www.huffingtonpost.com/entry/epa-spill-of-toxic-waste-could-be-long-term-calamity_us_55cbb9c9e4b064d5910a6abd.

48 Valentin Thurn, "Author: European Food Waste Adds to World Hunger," *Deutsche Welle*, March 25, 2012, http://www.dw.com/en/author-european-food-waste-adds-to-world-hunger/a-15837215.

49 "Michael Pollan Says: Take Back Control of Your Plate!," *Feedback*, accessed June 3, 2016, http://feedbackglobal.org/2014/10/830.

50–51 Dana Gunders, "Wasted: How America Is Losing Up to 40 Percent of Its Food from Farm to Fork to Landfill," Natural Resources Defense Council, August 2012, http://www.nrdc.org/sites/default/files/wasted-food-IP.pdf.

52 Jeff Nesbit, "World Leaders Are Fed Food Waste, and It's Great," *US News*, September 28, 2015, http://www.usnews.com/news/blogs/at-the-edge/2015/09/28/food-waste-is-an-environmental-problem.

52 Harish, "Animals We Use and Abuse for Food We Do Not Eat," Counting Animals, March 27, 2013, http://www.countinganimals.com/animals-we-use-and-abuse-for-food-we-do-not-eat.

54 Dan Barber, quoted in Nesbit, "World Leaders."

54 Amy Leibrock, "We Came, We Gleaned, We Fed Thousands," Sustainable America, October 21, 2014, http://www.sustainableamerica.org/blog/we-came-we-gleaned-we-fed-thousands.

55 Jordan Figueiredo, "The US Food Waste Revolution: Just Starting to Cook," Think.Eat.Save, accessed June 3, 2016, http://www.thinkeatsave.org/index.php?option=com_content&view=article&id=382.

58 Roma Eisenstark, "China's Rural Dumping Grounds," *Slate*, May 29, 2015, http://www.slate.com/articles/life/caixin/2015/05/china_s_waste_management_garbage_disposal_in_the_country_s_rural_areas_is.html.

60 Judy Li, "Ways Forward from China's Urban Waste Problem," Nature of Cities, February 1, 2015, http://www.thenatureofcities.com/2015/02/01/ways-forward-from-chinas-urban-waste-problem.

65 Tom Zeller Jr., "Few Rules for Recycling Electronics," *New York Times*, May 31, 2009, http://www.nytimes.com/2009/06/01/business/energy-environment/01iht-green01.html?scp=5&sq=electronic%20waste&st=cse.

65 Mike Anane, quoted in Jacobo Ottaviani, "E-Waste Republic," *Al Jazeera*, 2015, http://interactive.aljazeera.com/aje/2015/ewaste/index.html.

66 Unnamed worker, quoted in Bharati Chaturvedi, "Dismantling India's E-Waste: Potential for Green Jobs?," *Huffington Post*, last modified May 25, 2011, http://www.huffingtonpost.com/bharati-chaturvedi/dismantling-indias-e-wast_b_369218.html.

69 Jim Puckett, quoted in Basel Action Network, "Goodwill and Dell, Inc., Exposed as Exporters of US Public's Toxic Electronic Waste to Developing Countries," Basel Action Network, May 9, 2016, http://wiki.ban.org/images/b/bc/Goodwill_and_Dell%2C_Inc._Exposed_as_Exporters_of_US_Public%27s_Toxic_Electronic_Waste_to_Developing_Countries.pdf.

71 Charles J. Moore, quoted in Thomas Hayden, "Trashing the Oceans," *Mindfully.org* (blog), November 4, 2002, http://www.mindfully.org/Plastic/Ocean/Trashing-Oceans-Plastic4nov02.htm.

72 Chris Mooney, "Humans Are Putting 8 Million Metric Tons of Plastic in the Oceans—Annually," *Washington Post*, February 12, 2015, http://www.washingtonpost.com/news/energy-environment/wp/2015/02/12/humans-are-putting-8-million-metric-tons-of-plastic-in-the-oceans-annually/?tid=a_inl.

74 Susan Casey, "Garbage In, Garbage Out," *Oceans*, January 14, 2010, http://
conservationmagazine.org/2010/01/garbage-in-garbage-out.

74 Thomas Morton, "Toxic: Garbage Island," *Vice*, April 7, 2008, http://www.vice
.com/pt_br/read/toxic-garbage-island-1-of-3.

75 Frank Rocco, quoted in Nathaniel Berman, "6 Extraordinary Art Projects Use
Plastic Trash to Highlight the Crisis Facing the World's Oceans," *Alternet*, May
23, 2016, http://www.alternet.org/environment/6-extraordinary-art-projects-use
-plastic-trash-highlight-crisis-facing-worlds-oceans.

76 Denise Hardesty, quoted in Seth Borenstein, "Feed the Birds . . . Plastics,?" *US
News*, August 31, 2015, http://www.usnews.com/news/science/news/articles
/2015/08/31/whats-in-90-percent-of-seabirds-guts-1-word-plastics.

77 Hal Whitehead, ed., "Whalewatcher: Sperm Whale," *Journal of the American
Cetacean Society* 41, no. 1 (Spring 2012), http://www.pelagosinstitute.gr/gr
/erevnitika_programmata/pdfs/whalewatcher_%20sperm_whale.pdf.

78 Vibeke Venema, "The Dutch Boy Mopping Up a Sea of Plastic," *BBC News*,
October 17, 2014, http://www.bbc.com/news/magazine-29631332.

80 "Mr. Trash Wheel," Waterfront Partnership of Baltimore, accessed June 14,
2016, http://baltimorewaterfront.com/healthy-harbor/water-wheel.

80 Damon Beres, "This Group Wants to Build a Giant Barrier to Pull Trash from
the Pacific," *Huffington Post*, August 25, 2015, http://www.huffingtonpost.com
/entry/ocean-cleanup-group-launches-ambitious-plan-to-tidy-the-pacific_
us_55dc72f5e4b04ae497045d85.

84 Bridie Smith, "'Catastrophic Avalanche' of Space Junk Could Wipe Out
Satellites within Years," *Sydney Morning Herald*, May 31, 2016, http://www.smh
.com.au/technology/sci-tech/catastrophic-avalanche-of-space-junk-could-wipe
-out-satellites-within-years-20160531-gp8415.html.

84–85 Leonard David, "China's Anti-Satellite Test: Worrisome Debris Cloud Circles
Earth," *Space.com*, February 2, 2007, http://www.space.com/3415-china-anti
-satellite-test-worrisome-debris-cloud-circles-earth.html.

87 "Readying ESA's 'Garbage Truck': Robin Biesbroek Interview," ESA, March 21,
2014, http://www.esa.int/Our_Activities/Space_Engineering_Technology
/Clean_Space/Readying_ESA_s_garbage_truck_Robin_Biesbroek_interview.

88 Jonathan Missel, quoted in Leonard David, "'Sling-Sat' Could Remove Space
Junk on the Cheap," *Space.com*, March 1, 2013, http://www.space.com/20024
-space-junk-removal-sling-sat.html.

GLOSSARY

anthropogenic: resulting from the influence of human beings on nature. Most scientists say that climate change is anthropogenic—it results from people burning fossil fuels.

aquifer: an underground layer of water-bearing rock. Humans drill wells into aquifers to extract drinking water. Human trash, such as leachate from landfills and deep-well injection, sometimes contaminate aquifers.

benzene: a flammable toxic liquid, derived from petroleum, often used as a solvent and in motor fuel. Studies by the Environmental Protection Agency show that benzene can cause cancer and birth defects in humans.

biodegradable: capable of being broken down into harmless substances by bacteria and other living organisms. Organic materials, such as plant fibers and animal tissues, are biodegradable. Most materials made from petrochemicals, such as plastics, are not biodegradable.

biogas: a mixture of methane and carbon dioxide produced when organic matter decays. Energy companies use methane produced by decaying matter in landfills to make biogas.

carbon dioxide: a colorless gas found naturally in Earth's atmosphere. Human activities, such as burning fossil fuels and cutting down large stands of trees (which absorb carbon dioxide to make food), have increased the amount of carbon dioxide in the atmosphere. The excess carbon dioxide is trapping heat near Earth's surface and leading to higher temperatures and climate change.

climate change: a change in global and regional climate patterns brought on by the burning of fossil fuels. Burning fossil fuels releases excess carbon dioxide into the atmosphere. The carbon traps heat near Earth and leads to higher air and ocean temperatures, which in turn lead to Arctic melt and more extreme droughts, storms, and floods worldwide.

compost: decayed organic material, such as food scraps and yard waste, that can be used as a fertilizer for plants. Environmentalists encourage turning organic waste into compost rather than burying it in landfills.

deep-well injection (DWI): disposing of hazardous liquids by pumping them deep into underground caverns or between layers of impermeable rock. The process is designed to keep hazardous waste from contaminating air, soil, or water, but some DWI systems have leaked and contaminated soil and aquifers.

dioxin: any of a group of toxic hydrocarbons produced during industrial processes, such as papermaking and manufacturing plastics. Dioxin is a proven carcinogen and endocrine disrupter.

endocrine disrupter: a chemical that can interfere with the body's endocrine (hormone) system, leading to tumor growth, birth defects, abnormal sexual development, and other health problems. Many chemicals used in manufacturing, including dioxin and PCB, are proven endocrine disrupters.

energy-from-waste system: an incinerator that generates power by burning garbage. The heat from the incinerator boils water, which creates steam that spins mechanical turbines. The spinning turbines generate electricity that power companies provide to homes and businesses.

Environmental Protection Agency (EPA): a US government agency tasked with protecting human health and the environment by setting national standards to regulate toxic chemicals, landfills, and air and water pollution

e-waste (electronic waste): discarded electrical devices, such as computer monitors, smartphones, and printers, most of which contain valuable metals such as gold, silver, and copper

food chain: the flow of food in an ecosystem, usually with small organisms (such as plankton) being eaten by larger ones (such as fish), which are themselves eaten by even larger ones (such as humans). If organisms at the bottom of the food chain ingest toxic substances, the toxins can travel up the food chain to the bodies of organisms at the top.

food insecurity: the lack of regularly available food. This can lead to malnourishment when people regularly miss meals.

food waste: edible food that is available for human consumption but is not eaten

fossil fuels: the naturally occurring, carbon-based minerals coal, petroleum, and natural gas. When these substances burn, they release carbon dioxide into the atmosphere. Increasing levels of carbon dioxide on a massive scale have led to climate change on Earth.

garbologist: someone who studies trash to learn about the lives of the people who created the trash

Great Pacific Garbage Patch: a section of the North Pacific Ocean where swirling currents have pulled in tons of plastic garbage that originated either on land or with boats at sea

greenhouse gas: a gas such as methane and carbon dioxide that traps heat near Earth, in the same way that the glass roof of a greenhouse traps heat to warm the plants inside. The amount of greenhouse gases in the atmosphere has been increasing, leading to higher temperatures and climate change on Earth.

heavy metals: dense toxic metals such as cadmium, mercury, lead, nickel, cobalt, zinc, and copper. Small amounts of some heavy metals are essential to human health. But at high concentrations, heavy metals can poison plants and animals.

herbicide: a substance used to destroy or inhibit plant growth. Many farmers spray herbicides on their fields to kill weeds. Many herbicides contain trichlorophenol (TCP), a hydrocarbon that is also toxic to humans and other animals.

hydrocarbons: chemicals made of hydrogen and carbon that come from petroleum and natural gas. Manufacturers use hydrocarbons to create plastics and other synthetic substances. Many hydrocarbons are toxic.

hydrologist: a scientist who studies the circulation, behavior, and properties of water belowground, on Earth's surface, and in the atmosphere

incinerator: a furnace or container for burning waste

Kessler syndrome: the idea, first proposed by US astrophysicist Donald Kessler in 1978, that space junk creates more space junk. Kessler explained that when objects collide in space, they shatter into hundreds or thousands of fragments. Each of these fragments has the potential to hit other objects, in turn creating more space junk.

leach: to migrate out of a substance. For instance, toxic chemicals can leach from a plastic water bottle into the water inside the bottle. They can also leach from poorly maintained landfills.

leachate: a mix of wet, rotting food; chemical waste; and other liquids inside landfills. Leachate drains through the different layers inside a landfill to a network of pipes at the bottom. From there it is pumped to the surface and cleaned at water treatment plants.

materials recovery facilities (MRFs): waste treatment plants that use optical scanners to identify and sort reusable materials in garbage. MRFs send some of these materials, such as paper, metal, glass, and plastic, to recycling companies, which in turn make them into new products. MRFs also sort food waste from garbage and send it to be composted, or turned into fertilizer for farms and gardens.

methane: a greenhouse gas that contributes to climate change. Much of the excess methane entering the atmosphere comes from organic materials rotting in landfills. It also comes from the gas of the world's large cattle population.

microplastics: tiny bits of plastic created when large pieces of plastic break down because of exposure to sunlight

midden: a garbage heap, especially one left by ancient peoples. Archaeologists study ancient middens to learn about the daily life of those who created the garbage.

nurdles: tiny plastic pellets used to create plastic products. Nurdles are difficult to manage during transportation and manufacturing, and they can easily blow away in the wind and end up in bodies of water. Sea creatures sometimes accidentally ingest nurdles, thinking they are fish eggs or other food. The ingested nurdles then sicken and sometimes kill the animals.

orbital debris: sometimes called space junk, any human-made object traveling through space and not controlled by people on Earth

organic: derived from living or formerly living things, such as plant or animal tissue

pesticide: a chemical substance to kill insects. Farmers often spray pesticides on their fields to keep insects from damaging crops. Many pesticides contain chemicals that are also toxic to animals and humans.

petrochemicals: chemicals derived from petroleum or natural gas. Petrochemicals can be used to make many plastics and other synthetic substances and can also sicken humans and animals.

photodegradation: a process in which exposure to sunlight breaks plastic down into tiny particles

phthalates: endocrine disrupters found in many types of plastics that can lead to cancer and reproductive problems

plankton: tiny plants and animals that live in water and are a key food source for a wide variety of marine creatures. Plankton sometimes ingest plastics and other toxins, which then work their way up the food chain to larger organisms.

plastic: manufactured substances that can be shaped into almost any form. Most plastics are made by combining chemical compounds and are usually inexpensive to produce. Plastics can take hundreds or thousands of years to break down in the environment. When they do, they disintegrate into smaller and smaller bits of plastic and never actually disappear completely.

plate waste: uneaten food discarded after a meal

polychlorinated biphenyls (PCBs): heat-resistant hydrocarbons used in the twentieth century to make many industrial products, such as insulation, sealants, caulking, paint, and asphalt. The United States banned the use of PCBs in 1979 after they were found to cause birth defects, cancer, and other health problems.

polyethylene terephthalate (PET): a type of plastic used to make bottles for beverages. PET contains acetone, benzene, and other toxins, which can migrate from the plastic bottles into the beverages they contain and from there into the person who drinks them.

polymer: a large molecule formed by the chemical linking of smaller molecules into a long chain. Plastics are made of polymers.

polyvinyl chloride (PVC): a type of plastic commonly used to make plastic wrap, shower curtains, and children's toys. Scientists have linked PVC to cancer, birth defects, and other health problems.

recycling: the collection, processing, and repurposing of materials that otherwise would be thrown away. Commonly recycled materials include aluminum cans, glass containers, used office paper, and plastic containers. Communities may or may not have organized recycling programs, depending on how expensive the programs are.

sanitary landfill: an underground structure, with a lining of clay and polyethylene, built for the disposal of garbage. Each day workers at a well-regulated landfill cover the garbage deposited that day with soil. Pumps bring the leachate that drains through garbage to the surface for cleaning. Some landfills have wells that bring methane to the surface for use as biogas. In poor nations of the world, landfills are often open pits of waste.

space junk: also called orbital debris, any human-made object traveling through space that is not controlled by people on Earth

Superfund: a nickname for the US Comprehensive Environmental Response, Compensation, and Liability Act, passed in 1980, a program of government cleanup of hazardous waste sites. It is underfunded and not well regulated so it has been only partially successful.

zombie satellite: a satellite that is out of operation and no longer in communication with controllers on Earth

SELECTED BIBLIOGRAPHY

Beins, Kaley, and Stephen Lester. *Superfund: Polluters Pay So Children Can Play*. Center for Health, Environment & Justice, December 2015. http://chej.org/wp-content /uploads/Superfund-35th-Anniversary-Report1.pdf.

Dvorsky, George. "What Would Happen If All Our Satellites Were Suddenly Destroyed?" *Gizmodo*, June 4, 2015. http://io9.gizmodo.com/what-would-happen -if-all-our-satellites-were-suddenly-d-1709006681.

Eisenstark, Roma. "China's Rural Dumping Grounds." *Slate*, May 29, 2015. http:// www.slate.com/articles/life/caixin/2015/05/china_s_waste_management_garbage_ disposal_in_the_country_s_rural_areas_is.html.

Gunders, Dana. "Wasted: How America Is Losing Up to 40 Percent of Its Food from Farm to Fork to Landfill." National Resources Defense Council, August 2012. http://www.nrdc.org/sites/default/files/wasted-food-IP.pdf.

Hall, Eleanor. "Space Junk Poses Threat to Navigation and Communication Satellites." *ABC News*, May 31, 2016. http://www.abc.net.au/worldtoday/content/2016 /s4472628.htm.

Hayden, Thomas. "Trashing the Oceans." *Mindfully.org* (blog), November 4, 2002. http://www.mindfully.org/Plastic/Ocean/Trashing-Oceans-Plastic4nov02.htm.

Laskow, Sarah. "How the Plastic Bag Became So Popular." *Atlantic*, October 10, 2014. http://www.theatlantic.com/technology/archive/2014/10/how-the-plastic-bag -became-so-popular/381065

Lee, G. Fred, and Anne Jones-Lee. *Assessment of the Performance of Engineered Waste Containment Barriers*. Washington, DC: National Academies, 2009.

Leibrock, Amy. "We Came, We Gleaned, We Fed Thousands." Sustainable America, October 21, 2014. http://www.sustainableamerica.org/blog/we-came-we-gleaned -we-fed-thousands.

Lustgarten, Abrahm. "Injection Wells: The Poison Beneath Us." *ProPublica*, June 21, 2012. http://www.propublica.org/article/injection-wells-the-poison-beneath-us.

Nesbit, Jeff. "World Leaders Are Fed Food Waste, and It's Great." *US News*, September 28, 2015. http://www.usnews.com/news/blogs/at-the-edge/2015/09/28/food -waste-is-an-environmental-problem.

Ottaviani, Jacobo. "E-Waste Republic." *Al Jazeera*, 2015. http://interactive.aljazeera.com /aje/2015/ewaste/index.html.

Packard, Vance. *The Waste Makers*. London: Longmans, Green, 1961.

Simmons, Ann M. "The World's Trash Crisis, and Why Many Americans Are Oblivious." *Los Angeles Times*, April 22, 2016. http://www.latimes.com/world /global-development/la-fg-global-trash-20160422-20160421-snap-htmlstory.html.

Thurn, Valentin. "Author: European Food Waste Adds to World Hunger." *Deutsche Welle*, March 25, 2012. http://www.dw.com/en/author-european-food-waste-adds -to-world-hunger/a-15837215.

FURTHER INFORMATION

BOOKS

Bloom, Jonathan. *American Wasteland: How America Throws Away Nearly Half of Its Food (and What We Can Do about It)*. Boston: Da Capo, 2011.

Decker, Julie, ed. *Gyre: The Plastic Ocean*. London: Booth-Clibborn, 2014.

Donovan, Sandy. *Thrift Shopping: Discovering Bargains and Hidden Treasures*. Minneapolis: Twenty-First Century Books, 2015.

Freinkel, Susan. *Plastic: A Toxic Love Story*. New York: Houghton Mifflin Harcourt, 2011.

Hughes, Meredith Sayles. *Plants vs. Meats: The Health, History, and Ethics of What We Eat*. Minneapolis: Twenty-First Century Books, 2016.

Humes, Edward. *Garbology: Our Dirty Love Affair with Trash*. New York: Avery, 2012.

Kallen, Stuart A. *Running Dry: The Global Water Crisis*. Minneapolis: Twenty-First Century Books, 2015.

Lindner, Christoph, and Miriam Meissner, eds. *Global Garbage: Urban Imaginaries of Waste, Excess, and Abandonment*. New York: Routledge, 2015.

McPherson, Stephanie Sammartino. *Arctic Thaw: Climate Change and the Global Race for Energy Resources*. Minneapolis: Twenty-First Century Books, 2015.

Minter, Adam. *Junkyard Planet*. New York: Bloomsbury, 2013.

Moore, Charles. *Plastic Ocean: How a Sea Captain's Chance Discovery Launched a Determined Quest to Save the Oceans*. New York: Avery, 2012.

Newman, Patricia. *Plastic Ahoy! Investigating the Great Pacific Garbage Patch*. Minneapolis: Millbrook Press, 2014.

Smith, Rick. *Slow Death by Rubber Duck: The Secret Danger of Everyday Things*. Berkeley, CA: Counterpoint, 2011.

Stewart, Alison. *Junk: Digging through American's Love Affair with Stuff*. Chicago: Chicago Review, 2016.

Szaky, Tom. *Outsmart Waste: The Modern Idea of Garbage and How to Think Our Way Out of It*. San Francisco: Berrett-Koehler, 2014.

Szaky, Tom, and Albe Zakes. *Make Garbage Great: The Terracycle Family Guide to a Zero-Waste Lifestyle*. New York: HarperCollins, 2015.

Terry, Beth. *Plastic-Free: How I Kicked the Plastic Habit and How You Can Too*. New York: Skyhorse, 2015.

Young, Karen Romero. *Space Junk: The Dangers of Polluting Earth's Orbit*. Minneapolis: Twenty-First Century Books, 2016.

FILMS

Beijing Besieged by Waste. DVD. Beijing: Wang Jiu-liang Studio, 2011. Photographer Wang Jiuliang visited hundreds of illegal landfills circling Beijing and made this documentary about the city's out-of-control garbage crisis.

Garbage Dreams. DVD. New York: Iskander Films, 2009. This award-winning film follows three teenage boys born into a "garbage village," a community of trash pickers on the outskirts of Cairo, Egypt.

Trashed. DVD. Seattle: CustomFlix, 2007. Trashed is a provocative investigation of one of the fastest-growing industries in North America: the garbage business. The film examines the impact of garbage on US natural resources and explains why Americans produce so much garbage.

Waste Land. DVD. New York: Arthouse Films, 2011. Filmed over the course of three years, this movie follows artist Vik Muniz as he examines the lives of a group of Brazilian garbage recyclers at one of the world's largest dumps.

WEBSITES

Algalita Marine Research and Education
http://www.algalita.org
Charles J. Moore, the first person to encounter the Great Pacific Garbage Patch, founded this organization to bring attention to and research plastic trash in the world's oceans. The website features the latest news on plastic in the ocean, as well as blogs, videos, educational materials, and links to the group's research projects. Algalita also hosts the POPS International Youth Summit, which brings together students from around the world to fight for clean oceans.

Basel Action Network (BAN)
http://www.ban.org
The Basel Action Network works to end the international trade in e-waste and campaigns for a clean environment. BAN's website features investigative news stories, proposed solutions to the dangers of e-waste, and links to programs for responsibly recycling old electronics.

Becoming Minimalist
http://www.becomingminimalist.com
The website of minimalism proponent Joshua Becker provides information and tips about living with fewer possessions.

How the Oceans Can Clean Themselves: Boyan Slat at TEDxDelft
http://tedxtalks.ted.com/video/How-the-oceans-can-clean-them-2
This TEDx Talk features inventor Boyan Slat discussing his work tackling the problem of plastics in the ocean.

Reduce, Reuse, Recycle
http://www.epa.gov/recycle
This website, hosted by the Environmental Protection Agency, shows how consumers can reduce their garbage output and then save money and help the environment.

Seven Days of Garbage

http://www.greggsegal.com/7days.php

Gregg Segal created this photographic essay to call attention to the amount of waste an average family disposes of in a week. Striking photos show people from above, lying on the ground surround by their trash.

The Story of Stuff Project

http://storyofstuff.org

The Story of Stuff Project began with a twenty-minute movie about the production and disposal of all the consumer products we use each day. The project has expanded to include campaigns to protect water, land, and living things from toxic pollution.

Superfund365: A Site a Day

http://www.superfund365.org

Starting on September 1, 2007, Superfund365 visited one toxic Superfund site each day. The journey began in the New York City area and ended in Hawaii one year later. The website provides information on and pictures of 365 of the most toxic sites in the United States, roughly a quarter of those on the Superfund's National Priorities List.

Wasted Food

http://www.wastedfood.com

Jonathan Bloom, known as the Wasted Food Dude, hosts this website. It examines how Americans squander vast amounts of food. Part blog, part call to action, the site provides tips for saving food, food rescue information, and articles about food waste.

INDEX

PHOTO ACKNOWLEDGMENTS

The images in this book are used with the permission of: © Ratchat/Shutterstock.com, p. 1 (backgrounds); © iStockphoto.com/leonello, p. 1 (Earth); © iStockphoto.com/thawornnurak, p. 1 (closeup trash bag); © Citizen of the Planet/SuperStock, p. 4; © Paul Taggart/Bloomberg/Getty Images, p. 7; The Granger Collection, New York, pp. 9, 11; © PhotoQuest/Getty Images, p. 13; © Reciprocity Images/Alamy, p. 16; © Qamar Sibtain/India Today Group/Getty Images, p. 18; © Dmitry Kalinovsky/Shutterstock.com, p. 20; © Thomas Trutschel/Photothek/Getty Images, p. 22; © Laura Westlund/Independent Picture Service, pp. 23, 72; © Jason Smalley Photography/Alamy, p. 25; © Islandstock/Alamy, p. 30; © Brent Lewis/The Denve/Getty Images, p. 32; © Design Pics Inc/Alamy, p. 35; © Bloomberg/Getty Images, p. 37; © Paul Matzner/Alamy, p. 42; © SuperStock/Alamy, p. 46; © Fatih Aktas/Anadolu Agency/Getty Images, p. 48; © Jan Sochor/Latincontent/Getty Images, p. 50; Richard B. Levine/Newscom, p. 55; © STR/AFP/Getty Images, p. 58; REUTERS/Jason Lee, p. 60; REUTERS/Kim Kyung-Hoon, p. 62; © Thomas Imo/Photothek/Getty Images, p. 64; © Dhiraj Singh/Bloomberg/Getty Images, p. 66; © Lonely Planet Images/Getty Images, p. 70; © George Ostertag/Alamy, p. 75; © Westend61/Getty Images, p. 77; © REMKO DE WAAL/EPA/Redux, p. 79; NASA, pp. 82, 89; © Jwmissel/Wikimedia Commons (CC BY-SA 3.0), p. 87; NASA/NOAA/GSFC/Suomi NPP/VIIRS/Norman Kuring, p. 90; © imageBROKER/SuperStock, p. 91.

Front cover: © iStockphoto.com/leonello (Earth); © iStockphoto.com/Erdosain (garbage bag).

Back cover: © iStockphoto.com/thawornnurak (closeup trash bag).

ABOUT THE AUTHOR

Stuart A. Kallen has written more than 350 nonfiction books for children and young adults. His books have covered a wide arc of human history, culture, and science, from the building of the pyramids to the music of the twenty-first century. His recent titles include *Malala Yousafzai, Cutting Edge Entertainment Technology*, and *Running Dry: The Global Water Crisis*, a Children's Book Committee at Bank Street College Best Children's Book of the Year. Kallen, who lives in San Diego, California, is also a singer-songwriter and guitarist.